101 Weird Moments in Human History

Welcome Aboard, Check Out This Limited-Time Free Bonus!

Ahoy, reader! Welcome to the Ahoy Publications family, and thanks for snagging a copy of this book! Since you've chosen to join us on this journey, we'd like to offer you something special.

Check out the link below for a FREE e-book filled with delightful facts about American History.

But that's not all - you'll also have access to our exclusive email list with even more free e-books and insider knowledge. Well, what are ye waiting for? Click the link below to join and set sail toward exciting adventures in American History.

Access your bonus here

https://ahoypublications.com/

Or, Scan the QR code!

Table of Contents

Introduction

Have you ever found yourself utterly captivated by the fascinating oddities of human history? Have you ever been drawn to the stories that defy explanation, challenge conventional wisdom, and leave you utterly flabbergasted? If you're nodding your head in agreement, then you're in for a treat because "101 Weird Moments in Human History" is here to take you on an extraordinary journey through time.

In a world filled with history books that often delve into dry dates, endless genealogies, and intricate political maneuverings, "101 Weird Moments in Human History" stands out as a breath of fresh air. This book isn't about memorizing a list of monarchs or reciting endless battles. It's about diving deep into the strange, the unexpected, and the downright bizarre episodes that have shaped this world.

What sets this book apart from others in the genre is its accessibility. It's designed for anyone who has the slightest curiosity about history, from the seasoned history buff to the complete novice. It distills complex historical events into engaging, easy-to-understand narratives.

You'll impress your friends at dinner parties with tales of Stone Age stunts that defy belief or regale them with stories of how the ancient Egyptians had a secret side that would leave even the best Egyptologists scratching their heads. With "101 Weird Moments in Human History," you'll become the life of the party, armed with astonishing stories from the annals of history.

But it doesn't stop there. This book is not just about passive reading but active exploration. In addition to the engaging narratives, you'll discover hands-on methods and instructions that allow you to delve even deeper into these weird and wonderful moments. You'll be able to put yourself in the shoes of historical figures and experience their world firsthand, whether it's through bizarre rituals, peculiar inventions, or outlandish customs.

Picture yourself traveling back in time to the days of the Roman Empire, where you'll decipher the graffiti-laden walls of Pompeii or learn the tricks of the gladiator trade. Or step into the shoes of a Victorian-era inventor and tinker with steam-powered contraptions that will leave you in awe of their ingenuity. As you explore the world of these inventors, you'll discover that their creations were not only marvels of engineering but also reflections of the spirit of innovation that defined the age. It's a journey that will leave you inspired and amazed by the boundless creativity of the past.

"101 Weird Moments in Human History" is a passport to a world of strangeness, a time machine that will transport you to eras that will delight you. It's your gateway to discovering the remarkable, the astonishing, and the downright peculiar stories that have shaped this world.

So, if you're ready to be transported to a world where the unusual is the norm, where history is anything but dry, and where learning is as enjoyable as it is enlightening, then this book is for you. Get ready to embark on a remarkable adventure that will leave you with a newfound appreciation for the bizarre. Your next great historical adventure awaits!

Chapter 1: Stone Age Stunts (2,500,000-10,000 BCE)

The Stone Age is a hotbed of utterly insane weirdness. This period of human development is the longest in history, yet the world knows so little about it due to the poor record keeping of that time. It is easy to imagine the Stone Age as a stepping stone toward civilization, but the more that scientists discover, it becomes apparent that people of this period had complex societies with philosophical and spiritual understandings of their existence. Considering how long the Stone Age was, it makes sense that exploring this era will reveal a treasure chest of mind-shattering occurrences that are deeply seeped in mystery. Furthermore, there are captivating details that reveal the steps it took to get humanity to the civilized, interconnected, and global society that it is today.

As you dive down the rabbit hole of Stone Age existence, you will get a glimpse into the ancient past that evolutionarily shaped much of human behavior into the modern age. People are a bunch of weirdos because humanity's Stone Age ancestors were, in fact, weird. So, if you are looking for someone to put the blame on, turn and face about two million years ago. From artwork to religion, gender, and, best of all, good old-fashioned cannibalism, ancient humans were a fascinating bunch. Explore who laid the foundation for modern oddities, and discover how much and how little people have changed over thousands of years. See what the most intelligent animal on the planet was up to before the agrarian and industrial revolutions granted humanity the technology to build expansive civilizations. In the pockets of small tribal groups, some of the craziest and most surprising endeavors took place.

1. Cave Painting in Trois-Frères France

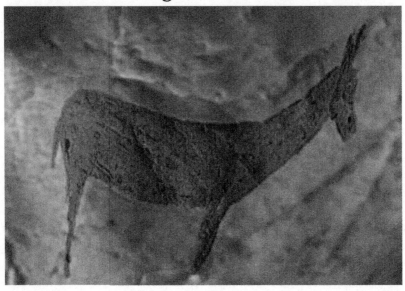

Painting in Trois-Frères cave.

For decades, archeologists believed that humanity was only able to develop deeper thought after the invention of agriculture. The theory was that in the distant past, humans were hunter-gatherers, which meant that their nomadic life always kept them busy, so they would be unable to ponder the abstract realities of the world. Agriculture allowed people to have more time on their hands because they did not have to constantly hunt, and they didn't have to follow the migrations of animals according to the season. New data has revealed that this view is incomplete. Humanity has always been drawn to interpreting the patterns they perceive in life through spiritual or philosophical lenses. One of the key pieces of evidence that suggests that it may be necessary to give cavemen a bit more intellectual respect is the cave paintings in Trois-Frères in France.

The paintings have several interesting figures, including weird animal-human hybrids. The cave was discovered in 1914, and the paintings have been dated to be older than 14000 years. What's interesting about these paintings is that they point toward early humankind having an imaginative and mythological mindset to dream up otherworldly creatures. Although archeologists are not sure exactly what the paintings mean, they reasonably assume that it was linked to some sort of religious tradition or shamanistic practices because deep inside the cave, they found what is assumed to be an altar dedicated to a lioness goddess. The altar was engraved with a lioness figure and contained some fascinating artifacts like shells, animal teeth, and flints. This cave helps to reimagine the ancient past, reframing the bumbling, animalistic depiction of cave people common in media to more thoughtful people who experienced deep, insightful, abstract thought.

2. Venus Figurines

On August 7th, 1908, a discovery was made in an excavation led by Josef Szombathy in Austria. A plump and busty feminine figure made of limestone, now named the Venus I figurine or The Venus of Willendorf, was dug up on the banks of the Danube. Two more statuettes were found, but these were created from ivory and were younger than the almost 30,000-year-old Venus I figurine. Nobody is exactly sure what these figures were used for, but because of the filled-out body shape, many assume that they were linked to fertility rights. Considering that much of the world is now conditioned to think of deities as male, it is surprising that some of the oldest religious artifacts show signs of female worship amongst humanity's oldest ancestors. This invokes so many questions about how humanity developed patriarchal religious orders if signs suggest that spiritual thinking deified women as the earliest gods.

What makes these figures so interesting is that they show that it is probable that humans have been thinking symbolically for thousands of years. This begs the question, how much does the ability to think abstractly affect humankind's evolutionary development? Just like curvy women grace social media feeds and billboards, ancient humans meticulously carved voluptuous figures that may have been honored similarly. Whether it was religious, superstitious, artistic, or decorative remains a mystery, but the statuettes do reveal that the creative drive of humanity reflected what individuals desired in art to immortalize what they appreciate. The Venus figurines are said to have been used for survival or fertility, so they are some of the oldest examples of how art embodies what humans love and fear.

3. Bone Flutes

Have you ever looked at a bone on your plate and thought to yourself that you could make some music with it? Most sane people in the modern age would not have a thought like this, but to people in the Stone Age, this way of think was completely normal. In the Hohle Fels cave, archeologists discovered flutes made out of mammoth ivory as well as swan bones. The nomadic hunter-gatherers clearly made sure that they wasted nothing and used every part of the animal, even if it was just for entertainment. What is even more compelling than the material they used for the creation of wind instruments is the fact that humans have been producing music for tens of thousands, if not millions, of years.

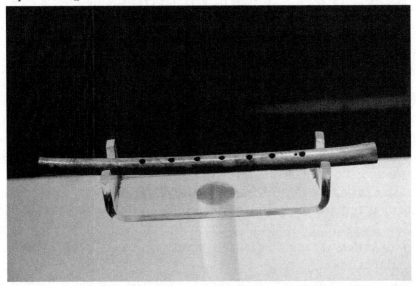

People in the Stone Age created flutes out of bones.
Gary Todd, CC0, via Wikimedia Commons:
https://commons.wikimedia.org/wiki/File:Early_Peiligang_Culture_Bone_Flute,_Wuyang.jpg

The instruments are a minimum of 35,000 years old. The bone flute had many holes, which meant that different notes could be played. This can make one wonder about the compositions that were produced in this era. Unfortunately, it is impossible to know how ancient human music sounded because there were no means of recording music at the time, even if it was just sheet notes written on paper. The carvings and paintings found near the same area may provide a glimpse into what they may have sung about. The natural world and its influence on human existence seem to be a common theme around this period. One can imagine a song about birds being sung with the accompaniment of a bone flute that comes from the body of the animal they are honoring. The intertwining of the pressing realities of life and death, even in art, is striking in prehistoric cultures.

4. Different Human Species

When people imagine the evolutionary chart, they tend to envision a neat march following one after the other, like in a tenth-grade biology textbook. However, the common view that is emerging now amongst that modern humans may have existed side by side with other hominin species. Neanderthals, Homo floresiensis, as well as the Denisovans all shared the planet with humans in their current form. These species of humans became extinct with time due to environmental factors. However, some claim that people interbred with these species, which could have contributed to their disappearance from the planet. Certain people have detectable Neanderthal DNA in their genes. So, instead of these other groups being distinct from people, they may have just become part of the family in some creatively intimate ways.

A variety of early human species have been found in Eurasia, Indonesia, and Siberia. The fossils of some of these species are over 100,000 years old. While – often – movies depict Neanderthals as dumb cavemen, it's possible they were highly intelligent with complex cultures and traditions. These species would be hardly distinguishable from modern humans, with so much overlap that they were able to interbreed. This view of human evolution erases the neatness of the common evolutionary chart and replaces it with a complex network of species and migrations that happened in an era before recorded history (so much of which has been lost to time!) As more discoveries get made, a clever picture of human origins will liekly begin developing. The collage of the formation of humans gets more captivating the more that is unearthed.

5. Drilling Holes in Living Skulls

Ancient neurosurgery free from anesthesia, safety considerations, or an understanding of bacteria is one of the most terrifying images that can cross one's mind. Picture laying down on a bed of leaves while four strong men hold you down as you kick and scream because someone is drilling a hole in your head with crude stone tools. Trepanation is the process of drilling a hole in a person's skull for medical reasons. The practice of trepanation dates back almost 10,000 years, with prehistoric skulls being found in France. This ancient practice helped build the most fundamental foundation of neurosurgery. The practice of trepanation continued all the way up until the 19th century. How nobody figured out that people should probably not be drilling holes in their heads for thousands of years is extremely shocking.

From the rocks of caves to the barbershop chair, then to the battlefield, and eventually to the comfortable, sterile hospitals society has today, surgery has come a long way. Some people theorize that cavemen drilled holes in skulls to treat headaches, but why that conclusion was reached escapes many because a crude drill to the skull seems like it will cause pain instead of relieve it. It is difficult to find out exactly why these prehistoric people practiced trepanation, but it was relatively common because 120 hole-filled skulls were unearthed in the French excavation. Be thankful for aspirin, considering the alternative is a literal hole in the head.

6. The Door Is on the Roof

As the name suggests, cave people are thought to have lived in caves. The later part of the Stone Age saw the development of closely packed mud homes. What makes these houses unique is that there were no doorways like people are used to today. Inhabitants had to climb down into their homes from a roof entrance. This was probably done as a way to avoid predators. The transition from caves to developing semi-permanent homes is a giant leap in the development of civilization. People at the time developed a network of alleyways between tightly packed living spaces so that they could easily move around their communal society. People navigated the crude pathways to move between houses and throw out any waste they had accumulated. They did not permanently stay in these mud homes because they were not yet in the agricultural age cultivating their produce and livestock; they still needed to move according to the migrations of their food sources.

It is interesting to think about how the design of mud homes switched from roof entrances to the doorways people have today. It is odd to envision coming home from a hard day's work and having to climb onto the roof and descend back down into your home. Necessity is the mother of invention, so with some investigation, it will one day be revealed exactly why this design choice was made. Perhaps the wood and mud structures were able to withstand the elements and provided people with a safe place to gather away from the constant natural danger that was common in the Stone Age.

7. Gender Equality

You would not be judged too much for assuming that the further you go back in time, the more oppressive and patriarchal cultures get. However, many of the nomadic hunter-gatherer societies of the ancient world were structured on egalitarian models. The average woman in the Stone Age era worked the same manual jobs as men and participated in hunting except when they were pregnant or nursing a young infant. These women were incredibly strong and could be compared to elite athletes in the modern age. When the focus was purely on survival, there was no time to establish oppressive hierarchies because life or death depended on the complete cooperation of the tribe. This egalitarian attitude is highlighted by the reality that the earliest deities that were mythologized were feminine, dealing with nature and fertility because those concepts directly impacted the tribe's daily life.

Patriarchal hierarchies may have begun forming when agriculture progressed. Why? Well, now there was ownership of land and a reason to expand or dominate. With ownership comes the need for governance, and in an era where brute force can be used to overpower people, women were considered typically physically weaker than men, thus easily falling subordinate to them. However, before that, the lives of cavewomen were relatively equal. You would expect cavemen to be more savage than their modern counterparts, but in some ways, they seemed to be more enlightened when it comes to gender equality. The philosophy and approach of equal rights that we are only beginning to unpack and explore in recent times were firmly a part of prehistoric society.

8. Home Swapping

Since prehistoric people built temporary homes, they simply abandoned the structure when they had to move on. They didn't always build homes when they settled in a new place. Sometimes, there would be homes that were left by other tribes that have moved on, so they would renovate these homes and live in them. This process was something like consensual squatting. During that time, there weren't any concepts of land ownership because the agrarian age had not yet flourished. Thus, cavepeople took *finders-keepers* to the next level by repossessing entire abandoned homesteads.

The small populations of humans at the time were likely to never bump into each other. These low numbers of humans were the same reasons that war was non-existent in the Stone Age. Humans died violent deaths, but seldom at the weapon of another person. People would never encounter the tribes that they were stealing from. The culture of hunter-gatherers was that you make do what is available . . . and if a fully formed structure is already available, it makes no sense to start fresh and build a new one!

9. Stone Age Bread

The savage misconception of how Stone Age people lived often creates this false memory of what prehistory meant. Meal time for ancient humans wasn't a man carrying a bloody carcass and dumping it onto a raging fire while guttural growling and screaming. There was some finesse and fine dining involved with some of humanity's oldest ancestors. Cave people baked flatbread. This is an amazing feat because of how labor-intensive it is to make bread. Other than the baking process itself, you would need to gather grains and grind them down before even being able to start.

Therefore, wholegrains and starch may have been part of the human diet for thousands of years. Food culture is not a modern invention. Tribes probably had foods and ways of preparation that were unique to them. Archeologists discovered that ancient humans made bread by finding remnants of the tasty treat in the ruins of an oven. The ingenuity of Stone Age people can never be understated when compared to the modern world, where many people would not survive a second with the comforts of contemporary society.

10. Cannibals

Cannibalism was not common among ancient humans, but the practice did occur. Big game animals were the primary source of protein for humanity's ancestors, but their attunement to the natural world meant that cave people were opportunistic. If there was the need to defend territory from a stranger, or if someone in the tribe died of natural causes, they would probably have gotten eaten in some cases, especially if hunts were unsuccessful. People do not go around hunting humans to eat because, as a prey animal, other people are too cunning and difficult to catch. However, if meat falls in your lap, what else can you do besides eat it?

Thinking about eating a fellow person is stomach-turningly disgusting, but if you lived on the edge of life and death where you were in the middle of the food chain eating and getting eaten, letting meat go to waste could seem foolish. Cannibalism was just the resourcefulness of what the environment required. Someone was probably making the argument that the tribe should not bury a fellow caveman, let's call him Steve, highlighting how he is a bit chunky and would go down well with a side of lettuce. The next man would be carrying Steve to the shade so that the meat wouldn't spoil too quickly before tonight's supper.

11. Ancient Dentistry

If the skull drilling wasn't horrifying enough, imagine taking your seat on a log in front of a wilderness dentist. Stone tools were used to scratch the decay out of cavities to relieve pain and prevent the tooth from rotting further. The bush dentist would then apply bitumen, a tar-like substance found in nature, as a filling. What makes this ancient dentistry so weird is that the techniques used today, although more sophisticated, are still similar to the ancient method because modern dentists drill into cavities and install fillings as well. People still dread going to the dentist now, so what would it be like without hygiene standards and painkillers while using crude tools?

The ancient dentist's masterful work was discovered in Northern Italy when archeologists uncovered teeth that seemed to have been worked on. Some plant matter and hair were also found in the fillings – but researchers are unsure about the purpose of including these contents! The roots of dentistry go back to the late Stone Age. Before this discovery, a wax filling was the oldest specimen that had been found in Pakistan. The Stone Age dental work shows that people have cared for their teeth for longer than civilization existed. Dentistry is older than the invention of the modern city.

Questions to Reflect on

1. What materials would be best suited for building a semi-permanent home as hunter-gatherers?

2. How do you think uneven societies developed when ancient cultures were highly egalitarian?

3. Why do you think ancient people did not commonly eat human meat, even though they were not against cannibalism?

4. Why do you think that people have this misconception that cavepeople were savages without deep philosophies and cultures?

5. What do you think cavepeople believed about their place in the universe since they did not have any written records that could be explored or interpreted?

Chapter 2: Strange Tales of Ancient Egypt (3100-30 BCE)

What comes to mind when you think of Ancient Egypt? You probably think of the Great Pyramids of Giza, the Sphinx, or mummies. Undoubtedly, Egypt is one of the oldest and richest cultures in the world. With a long history and 5,000 years of civilization, there is so much to tell about this ancient country. Luckily, its history is immortalized in many stories. Some are romantic, like the love story between King Akhenaten and his wife Nefertiti, while others are tragic, like the story of Isis and Osiris.

When you think of Ancient Egypt, you may think of the Great Pyramids of Giza and the Sphinx.
Most likely Hamish2k, the first uploader, CC BY-SA 3.0

Looking closely at Egyptian mythology, you will also find some strange and even creepy stories that will make you say, "Wait a minute, this can't be real."

Are you ready to take a journey back in time and discover the strangest tales of Ancient Egypt?

12. The Dwarfs of Pharaoh's Court

Pepi II Neferkare was an Egyptian pharaoh who ruled Egypt at the young age of six. Since he was just a child, a governor named Harkhuf – who had a great relationship with the young king – was appointed. Harkhuf was also an explorer who went on many expeditions in various countries around the world. He would always bring Pepi gifts from the fascinating places he visited.

When Pepi was eight years old, Harkhuf wrote him a letter describing the many gifts he brought him. However, there was one that caught the young king's attention, it was a dwarf that lived in the land of the spirits. For a moment, Pepi forgot he was a king and showed great excitement for his gift. He sent his governor a letter to return home as fast as he could.

Pepi also said in his letter that when they get on the boat, Harkhuf should appoint men to protect the dwarf at all times because he was worried he might fall overboard. He also told him that the men should check on him ten times at night while he was sleeping. Pepi promised Harkhuf a large reward if he brought the dwarf safe and healthy.

So why was Pepi so excited about his gift? The pharaohs held dwarfs in very high regard because they believed they were magical creatures who had powers and were associated with the gods. They even played a big role in many religious ceremonies where they performed and danced. For this reason, they were called "Dancers of the Gods."

Ancient Egyptian Kings loved owning dwarfs. When their dwarfs died, they held expensive funerals for them and buried them in luxurious graves.

One of the most famous dwarfs was called "Seneb." He has been immortalized in a statue with his wife and children, and it is believed that he was either born into a noble family or held a high position. There were many titles found in his tomb, including "Overseer of Dwarfs" and "Beloved of the King."

Khnumhotep was another well-known dwarf in the sixth dynasty. He has also been immortalized in a statue with his biography written on its base. He was a priest who performed rituals for the dead, including dancing at funerals. Another famous dwarf was Djeho, who was clearly beloved by his patron since they were buried in the same tomb. His sarcophagus was made of granite and clearly very expensive reflecting his sacred role as a dancer in burial rituals.

13. The Pharaoh Who Became a God

The Ancient Egyptians were polytheistic as they worshiped many gods and goddesses. No one ever thought of changing the status quo until the Pharaoh Akhenaten came to power.

Akhenaten wasn't an ordinary ruler, and he accomplished so much in his 17 years as a king, especially in the arts. However, nothing stood out more than revolutionizing the religious movement in Ancient Egypt. He introduced the idea of monotheism and called for his people to worship the sun god, Aten. He believed there wasn't any other deity as special, unique, or worthy of worship than the god of the sun. Only one person knew Aten and was allowed to speak to him and for him, and that person was Akhenaten.

Akhenaten had an ulterior motive, as he wanted to be the most powerful man in the world by being both a king and a prophet. He even created various false narratives and claimed it was the word of their god. Interestingly, the pharaoh was originally called Amenhotep, but he changed it to Akhenaten, meaning "one is effective for the Aten," to reflect his unique relationship with the god.

He also ordered his men to destroy all the statues and images of all the other gods. Akhenaten devoted a whole city to the worship of Aten and built many temples in the god's name. He called it "Akhetaten," meaning "The Horizon of the Aten." Akhenaten took an unprecedented step by telling artists to change the way he and his family were portrayed in paintings. He wanted to be depicted as androgynous with elongated bodies, making them larger and more superior to humans.

When the Ancient Egyptians saw these paintings, they felt that Akhenaten and his family weren't regular human beings, but divine creatures who were related to Aten.

14. The Mystery of the Screaming Mummy

In 1881, a team of archaeologists was unwrapping 50 mummies of royals discovered at Deir El-Bahari in Egypt. Everything seemed normal as they inspected one mummy after the other, but soon, they discovered something that horrified everyone present. They found a mummy that was unlike the rest. It belonged to a young man who had a horrified expression on his face and seemed to be screaming. Upon further investigation, they found something even more shocking. The mummy didn't have an incision. So why was that a problem?

The Ancient Egyptians made an incision on the left abdomen of the body to remove the organs during the mummification process. This showed that this mummy wasn't properly mummified. However, other strange things bewildered archaeologists.

The young man was covered in sheepskin, which was a symbol of disgrace in Ancient Egypt. This indicated that he committed a horrendous crime. He was also wearing gold earrings, which showed that he was of high status, possibly a prince. His hands and feet were bound.

So, who was this man? What was his story? Why was he screaming?

There were many theories behind this intriguing mummy, which was named "Unknown Man E." Archeologists first believed that he was poisoned, while others said that he was buried alive. Either way, his death was obviously painful, and it left him screaming for his life. However, the theories didn't stop there.

Some speculated that he was a foreign prince who came to Egypt to marry the widow of Tutankhamun. However, he was murdered, and his body was never found. So, it made sense that he was buried in an unmarked grave.

In 2012, scientists ran a DNA analysis and finally solved the mystery of "Unknown Man E." The corpse didn't belong to the foreign prince as initially thought. The screaming mummy was Prince Pentawer, the son of King Ramesses III. He plotted to kill his father and take his throne, but he was caught and sentenced to death.

The Judicial Papyrus of Turin mentioned his trial and revealed interesting facts about him. They called him "Pentawer, who bore that other name," so Pentawer wasn't his real name. They changed it to erase him from history as punishment for his treason. The papyrus also revealed that he was forced to commit suicide, and it is believed that he hung himself. This was a privilege given to him for his royal status.

He wasn't allowed mummification or a proper burial to prevent him from reaching the afterlife. However, it is clear that someone from high status gave him a quick mummification so his body wouldn't decay.

So how was he buried with kings and queens, including his father, Ramesses III? There was a time in Ancient Egypt when grave robbery was pretty common. They opened royal graves, took their valuables, and reburied them in Deir el-Bahri, where they would be discovered 3000 years later.

15. The Disappearance of Nefertiti

Nefertiti is one of the most famous and powerful queens from Ancient Egypt. Whether you are familiar with the pharaohs or not, you definitely know her name. But do you know how she died or where she is buried? Well, don't feel too bad about not knowing because no one actually knows. In fact, this once-powerful Queen disappeared from history, leaving behind many unanswered questions.

Nefertiti is one of the most famous queens from Ancient Egypt.
Arkadiy Etumyan, CC BY-SA 3.0 <http://creativecommons.org/licenses/by-sa/3.0/>, via Wikimedia Commons: https://commons.wikimedia.org/wiki/File:Nefertiti_30-01-2006.jpg

Nefertiti was one of the most beautiful women at the time. She was married to Akhenaten, and they had six daughters together. The couple was very much in love and devoted to each other, as it was clear in Akhenaten's poetry. However, things changed after the death of their Meketaten, which left them both heartbroken.

There is no mention of Nefertiti in any historical record after this tragic incident. However, there are a few theories that might explain her disappearance. The first theory was that Akhenaten abandoned her because she couldn't give him a male heir. However, many disputed it since Akhenaten had a son with his other wife, Kiya, so he didn't have a reason to leave her.

It was also believed that he banished her because she left the cult of Aten. However, there are no records to support this theory. Some believe that she committed suicide after she lost her daughter, but there is evidence that she was alive after Meketaten's passing. The last and most intriguing theory was that she changed her name to Smenkhkare and continued ruling Egypt after her husband died. She waited until Akhenaten's legitimate heir, Tutankhamun, was old enough, and then she stepped down.

No one knows for sure if any of these theories are true. The question of what happened to Nefertiti after the death of her daughter remained unanswered. No one knows when or how she died or where she was buried.

16. The Tragic Story of Isis and Osiris

Isis and Osiris's story is one of the first tragic love stories in history, even though many parts of their tale were quite strange. Isis was the goddess of healing and magic, and Osiris was the god of agriculture and fertility. They were brother and sister and husband and wife. This isn't the strange part, as this was normal at the time.

When their father, Geb, god of the Earth, decided to retire, he chose his eldest son, Osiris, to take his place. Osiris was a wise man and he and his wife were fair rulers and loved by all their people.

During times of famine, the Ancient Egyptians resorted to cannibalism. However, Osiris convinced them to forgo this uncivilized lifestyle and introduced farming and a moral code that the people lived by, and they all led a much happier and more peaceful life.

Sadly, this didn't last long. While Osiris was a handsome, just, and wise man, his brother Set was the complete opposite. He was evil, jealous, envious, and ugly. He hated his brother for many reasons, but the one reason that drove him to the edge was his wife, Nephthys, also their sister, having an affair with Osiris.

Set decided to kill Osiris by making a coffin that was the exact size of his brother – and then played a cruel trick on him. During a banquet, he challenged Osiris to get into the coffin, and if he fit inside, the coffin was his. Osiris trusted his brother and jumped into it. Set quickly sealed the coffin and threw it in the Nile. Osiris suffocated and died, and Set became King!

When Isis received the news, she was heartbroken over the loss of the man she loved. She decided to look for her husband and bring him back to life. When Set found out, he brought his brother's body, cut him into 42 pieces, and spread them all over Egypt to make her mission impossible.

However, Isis didn't give up. With the help of her sister Nephthys, they managed to collect 41 pieces, and Isis constructed the last missing piece. She revived Osiris for a short time so she could make love to him. She wanted to get pregnant so her son would take his father's place as king. Her plan worked, and she gave birth to a baby boy named Horus. Osiris was neither dead nor alive, so he became the god of the underworld.

17. The Creation Myth

Do you know how the universe was created in Ancient Egyptian mythology? Well, if you are looking for a weird story, it doesn't get any weirder than the creation myth.

Atum, also called Ra, was the first Egyptian god, and he came to be by willing himself to life and rising out of water. He was the only living being in the universe. There were no human beings or gods, as the world wasn't created yet.

Atum got lonely and bored, so he thought about making more gods to keep him company. However, this was tricky since he was alone and had no one to copulate with to start a family of deities. So, he decided to breed with his shadow.

When it was time to give birth, Atum struggled since he was a male. He found that his best option was to spit out his children Shu, god of air, and Tefnut, goddess of moisture. He then began creating the universe by masturbating.

However, a different version of the creation myth states that Shu and Tefnut created the Earth, and mankind was created from Ra's tears. Shu and Tefnut left Atum to explore the universe. He was sad and lonely when his children were gone. They later returned, and he was so happy to see them that he cried tears of joy, transforming into human beings.

18. The Eye of Ra (Myth 1)

Judging from the previous story, you can tell that Ra was a fascinating god, so he should be featured in more than one tale. The Eye of Ra was a popular symbol among the Ancient Egyptians. You are probably familiar with it as it is engraved in many Egyptian monuments, and many people also wear it as jewelry or get it tattooed on their bodies. So, what makes this symbol so popular? Well, there is more than one myth about this intriguing eye. Considered to be the female counterpart to Ra, the Eye of Ra was an extension of his powers.

Shu and Tefnut went to explore the universe their father had created. However, they didn't return, and Ra was worried and heartbroken. He was alone, and they were his only family. So he took out his eye and sent her after his children, hoping she would find them and return them to him.

Luckily for Ra, she succeeded in her mission and brought the gods safely to their father. However, in her absence, Ra couldn't see very well without his eye, so he grew another one. When the first eye returned, she was shocked to find she had been replaced. This was an unforgivable betrayal that hurt and upset her.

However, Ra wasn't pleased to see his eye feeling this way, so he turned her into a uraeus to wear over his forehead.

19. The Eye of Ra (Myth 2)

The second myth of the Eye of Ra is different since, in this tale, the eye isn't the hero but the *villain* of the story.

After Ra created the universe and mankind, he watched them from the heavens. He wasn't pleased with their actions, and in time, his wrath took over, and he decided that they must be punished. He sent his eye to slaughter them all.

The eye obeyed and killed many human beings, almost annihilating all mankind. When he saw the destruction he caused, Ra regretted his actions right away. However, the eye was out of control, so he decided to trick her.

He disguised beer as blood to fool her, and she drank until she passed out and was able to calm down and see the error of her ways. When she woke up, she returned to Ra, who transformed her into Sekhmet, the goddess of war, chaos, and plague.

20. The Story Behind Perfumes

Who doesn't love perfumes? They come in different scents, and they're known to make you feel like your best self! However, if you find out where the Ancient Egyptians think perfumes come from, you will change your mind about your love of perfumes.

The Ancient Egyptians believed that perfumes were made from Ra's sweat. So, applying perfume wasn't only hygienic but a religious act. It was like applying a holy liquid or a part of Ra on their body.

Perfumes played a big part in their lives, and they even assigned a god to it called Nefertum.

21. Electricity in Ancient Egypt

Did the Ancient Egyptians discover electricity? According to some researchers, yes. On the walls of the temple of Dendera, one of the most fascinating and mysterious images in Ancient Egypt was engraved. It is an illustration of a snake in a big ball of fire coming out of a lotus flower. Interestingly, this image resembles one of Crookes tube models – an early experimental light bulb invented in the *19th century!*

Many researchers believe this image proves that the Ancient Egyptians discovered and used electricity. If this is true, the Ancient Egyptians were way ahead of their time. Judging by the monuments they left and the many mysteries they left behind, the Ancient Egyptians were brilliant people, so it wouldn't come as a surprise if this theory was true.

22. Anubis, the Collector

Anubis was the god of mummification in Ancient Egypt. He supervised the process of preserving the corpse and led the spirits of the dead to the Hall of Truth, where they would receive their final judgment. However, Anubis had a very peculiar habit. He enjoyed collecting trophies (organs) from the people he helped mummify. When Set killed Osiris and cut his body, he offered his organs to Anubis as a gift.

Anubis was the god of mummification in Ancient Egypt.

For hundreds of years, the Ancient Egyptians offered dead bodies to Anubis. Many believe this was the reason he was depicted with a jackal's head. One can't help but compare Anubis to a modern-day serial killer who likes to keep trophies of his victims.

23. Apep and Ra

Apep was the god of chaos and was depicted as a large snake. He was also the biggest enemy of Ra, and the sun god was terrified of him for he represented chaos, darkness, and evil. In one legend, Apep swallowed Ra. Since he was the god of the sun, this left the world dark and scary. Luckily, the other gods cut a hole in Apep's stomach and freed Ra to save the world from darkness.

The battle between the two would go on until the end of time. If Apep succeeded in devouring Ra, Egypt would be dark forever. This would explain why Apep was called "The Evil Lizard."

Ancient Egypt is filled with strange stories and even stranger mysteries. Perhaps one day, with the help of technology, the world will finally get some answers. For now, one can only enjoy the unknown and imagine scenarios of all the possibilities.

Question to Reflect on:

1. Do you think the screaming mummy is really Prince Pentawer, the son of King Ramesses III, or will researchers discover something different in the future?

2. What do you think really happened to Nefertiti? Is it possible she wasn't a significant queen, as many believe? (And this may be why she easily disappeared from history?)

3. If you had the choice, would you bring a loved one back to life, like Isis did with Osiris?

4. What do you think of Ra's decision to destroy mankind that he created?

5. Do you think the Ancient Egyptians invented electricity, or are people just misinterpreting this image?

Chapter 3: Graffiti, Gladiators, and Gobbledygook: The Roman Empire's Strangest Stories (753 BCE - 476 AD)

The largest empire of the bygone era. A domineering supremacy. A long, authoritative rule. The ruthless emperors. The violent politics. A peaceful reign. A transformative period in human history. When the Roman Empire is the topic of discussion, grand descriptions like these come to mind. Indeed, the Roman Civilization lasted for more than 10 human lifespans, and the Empire reigned supreme for a little over 400 years. It was defined by its unbelievable 200-year-long peace (*Pax Romana*), followed by a longer period of internal animosity, bloody strife, incessant invasions, an empire-wide economic collapse, and the deadly Plague of Cyprian.

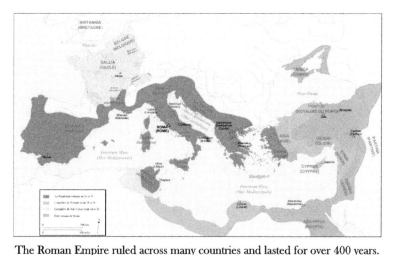

The Roman Empire ruled across many countries and lasted for over 400 years.
User:Historicair um15:17, 13 August 2007 (UTC), CC BY-SA 3.0
<http://creativecommons.org/licenses/by-sa/3.0/>, via Wikimedia Commons:
https://commons.wikimedia.org/wiki/File:Map_of_the_Ancient_Rome_at_Caesar_time_(with_co nquests)-fr.svg

It's time to change the general perception of this famous (or infamous, depending on perception) Empire from grandiose to a bit modest and humorous. The unusual Romans. Their hilarious antics. Their absurd laws. The Romans were humans, after all, prone to faults and quirks aplenty. However, since they enjoyed such a long and prosperous reign, their eccentricities were usually grander, often comical, and sometimes bizarre.

24. The Whispers of Pompeii

The Temple of Jupiter in Pompeii.
Jebulon, CC0, via Wikimedia Commons:
https://commons.wikimedia.org/wiki/File:Temple_of_Jupiter_side_view_Pompeii.jpg

To historians and history buffs, the Romans may seem like gods hailing from another universe. The ancient city of Pompeii proves that they were nothing more than humans. Pompeii was once a bustling city in the Roman Empire located near what is now called Naples, Italy. It sat near the base of the ferocious volcano, Mount Vesuvius, just around nine miles from its summit. One fine day in 79 CE, the volcano erupted in a bubbling stream of magma and devoured the entire city along with the surrounding territories.

It's considered to be one of the most devastating events in history, which claimed the lives of several thousand people (estimated 16,000). One good thing came out of this catastrophic incident, however, it preserved some unique eccentricities of the Romans. When Pompeii was first rediscovered in 1748, it was like finding a gold mine in a minefield. The sheer and dark destruction was glimmering with tiny nuggets of interesting information. It provided a singular insight into regular Roman life.

Today, people visit the dilapidated remains of Pompeii not to marvel at ancient Roman architecture but to gape at the zany graffiti on its walls and whispers of a time long past. From sweet declarations of love to heartfelt obituaries, the whispers often bordered on the obscene too. The language was primarily Latin. Here are a few intriguing and downright hilarious translations (family-friendly, of course).

"Go hang yourself!" was signed by Samius, dedicated to Cornelius.

"Cruel Lalagus, why do you not love me?"

"I'm sorry to hear you're dead, and so, goodbye," Pyrrhus's eulogy to Chias.

"Aufidius was here. Goodbye."

"Health to you, Victoria, and wherever you are, may you sneeze sweetly."

Epaphra was insulted several times. The most decent insult is, "Epaphra is not good at ball games." It probably refers to a social gathering.

Other graffiti included a lot of screws, sticks, and bread, a treat for vulgar minds.

25. Caligula's Horse Senator

Caligula was the most scandalous Roman Emperor and among the most morally warped individuals in human history. His infamous reign is rife with tales of blasphemy and debauchery, so much so that his name has become synonymous with incest. His perverted stories are bound to induce a cringe in the vilest of the vile, but there is one account that will make even a humorless person laugh their head off.

It is said that Caligula's love for animals far surpassed his affection for his fellow humans (he used to feed his prisoners to wild beasts). There was one animal in particular that he loved the most: his horse, Incitatus. He built a pristine marble cell for the stallion, wrapped a gem-studded collar around its neck, and in its later years, invited it to live in his domus (house).

As rumors of the madness of Caligula went, this behavior seemed sane in comparison. Then, as if to live up to his own expectations, he planned to make Incitatus a consul, the highest political office in the Empire, second to the Emperor himself.

However, before he could implement his plan, he was assassinated by one of his personal bodyguards, Cassius Chaerea. Certain accounts say that Chaerea was fulfilling a prophecy that went something like this, "be the horse that will kill Caligula." It's entirely possible that Chaerea killed his Emperor because of Incitatus.

26. Vestal Virgins and the Sacred Geese

In Roman religion, Vesta is the goddess of home and family, who, ironically, is a virgin. Her acolytes were called Vestal Virgins because they vowed to serve the goddess for at least 30 years after their initiation (just after puberty). During that time, they wouldn't have intimate relations with any man.

Interestingly, most Vestals remained virgins even after the 30-year span, continuing to serve their goddess. Granted, they were awarded many exclusive privileges for upholding their faith, so that could be one of the reasons. Who wouldn't want to be among the most powerful women in the land? Either way, it was because of their dedication to maintaining the sacredness of the Roman gods and goddesses that indirectly helped the Roman Republic thwart an invasion.

The year was 387 BCE, and the invasion of the Republic by the Senones, a now-extinct Gallic tribe, had culminated in the Battle of the Allia (near the Allia brook around 10 miles north of Rome). The Gauls became victorious, and Rome was in complete disarray. As the invaders marched toward the capital, the residents of the city hurried to evacuate. In stark contrast, the Vestal Virgins calmly stood guard around the sacred treasures of their gods and goddesses, hoarded in a temple atop a hill.

A few of these treasures included the sacred geese, which nested just outside the temple gates. Many of the armed defenders of Rome stayed in the temple to guard the Vestals and the other priests. They were tired and hungry, for all their food sources had been depleted. The thought of eating the geese hadn't even entered their minds because the Vestals held them so sacred.

By that time, the Gauls had stepped into the city's confines. A part of their army was trying to sneak their way into the temple. As soon as they reached the top of the hill, the geese started flapping their wings and screeching loudly, alerting the invaders' presence to the guards within. The guards immediately rushed outside and slammed their shields into the first row of the Gauls, who had just reached the top. They toppled backward onto the second row of the climbing soldiers until, one after the other, the entire battalion fell back down the hill like a set of dominoes.

If the Vestals hadn't protected their sacred geese, they would have been eaten by the defenders, and the invaders would have surrounded the temple and taken control of Rome.

27. The Rockstar Gladiators

The Roman gladiator bouts have become the stuff of legend. Its fictional adaptations (movies, TV shows, and books) have garnered a massive cult following over the years. They are also considered to be role models among many children. However, back in the day, the emperors and nobles only saw them as entertainment, pieces of flesh for spilling blood in the arena. Most of them were slaves. Nevertheless, among the masses and lower classes, they were rockstars.

Similar to the rockstars and celebrities of today, the portraits of the toughest gladiators were hung on home walls, children cuddled with their clay action figures before hitting the hay, and they were even hired as ambassadors to promote many products. Imagine a muscular guy garbed in gladiator armor, parading the streets outside the Colosseum, complete with a sword in one hand and a can of the world's finest olive oil (according to the manufacturers) in the other.

28. Exhibition Matches

Gladiator fights were always vicious and bloody. Like an exhibition match in a sports game, there were staged fights, too. Over time, the emperors and nobles realized how much gladiators mattered to the masses. Many of the top gladiators literally had a fan following bordering on idol worship. To win the hearts of their people, the rulers eventually started entering the arena themselves, donning rich gladiator robes and fine weaponry.

Their bouts were mostly staged, even if they squared off against real gladiators instead of fellow nobles, but if they were willing to enter the arena and endure a few bruises just to win the love of their people, their efforts should be commended, right? Not quite. When the names on the list of imperial gladiators included the likes of Caligula and Commodus, it's understood they didn't fight for the love and respect of their subjects but to satiate their own bloodlust.

29. The Nefarious Singing Ruler

Many historians believe Caligula to be the worst Roman Emperor, but he did the things he did because he suffered from mental health problems. His nephew and future Emperor, Nero, on the other hand, was pure evil. His administrative corruption and imperial failings were the least of his sins. His acts of sadism and violence are well known. It is rumored that he had intimate relations with his own mother, and he killed his wife when she found out about it. However, very few people know that he had dreams of becoming a singer and a musician.

Emperor Caligula is believed by many to be the worst Roman Emperor.
*Sergey Sosnovskiy from Saint-Petersburg, Russia, CC BY-SA 2.0
<https://creativecommons.org/licenses/by-sa/2.0>, via Wikimedia Commons:
https://commons.wikimedia.org/wiki/File:Caligula.Carlsberg_Glyptotek.(cropped).jpg*

During the inauguration of an amphitheater that Nero had ordered to be built, he started singing in a high-pitched operatic voice (at least, he believed it was an operatic voice). Soon after, the pregnant women in the theater began screaming as they gave birth, and the men fell to their deaths from the stalls.

But Nero wasn't one to give up. Despite the massacre his singing wrought in the theater, he continued to practice music. One day, when Rome was ablaze all around him (the great fire of 64 CE), he remained calm and started playing the fiddle. He wasn't crazy, however, just a sociopath of the highest order.

30. The Epileptic Vampires

They say that tales of blood-drinking vampires originated in the 18th century. However, the practice of consuming human blood began long before that, back during the Roman era. It wasn't some ghost story told to frighten children. Believe it or not, the practice was recommended by doctors as an alternative medicine.

Epileptic seizures were quite unusual back then. There wasn't any remedy for the disease, and the Roman doctors didn't really understand it. Noticing that gladiators were never afflicted with epilepsy, they came to the conclusion that the cure lay in the physiology of the combatants. Naturally, they prescribed drinking gladiator blood to treat the condition. Eating their liver was also recommended to relieve the seizures.

Contrary to popular belief, not many gladiators died in bouts. When fight events were organized, around 13-15 gladiators participated, and only about two or three of them fought to the death. People with epilepsy were far more common than that, but the dead gladiator's blood was enough for only a few of them. It is entirely possible that one of the remaining epileptics prowled the streets of Rome in the dark of the night, scouring the houses for gladiators to kill to suck their blood. The legend of vampires may have been born then, over 1500 years ago.

31. The Bizarre Elixir of Life

Mithridates used his elixir to live for over 80 years.
O.Mustafin, CC0, via Wikimedia Commons:
https://commons.wikimedia.org/wiki/File:Mithridates_VI.jpg

In Roman times, medicine was in its infancy, and epidemics and plagues ran rampant in the region. Amidst the fear and chaos of getting infected with diseases, Mithridates the Great came up with a bizarre idea (or was it a stroke of genius?). He brewed up a concoction that consisted of tiny amounts of every affliction he could lay his hands on, and he drank it as if it were the elixir of life.

It is said that Mithridates lived for over 80 years, healthy as a horse. His immunity-boosting concoction later came to be known as Mithridatium, and many Romans consumed it, hoping to prolong their life. Whether or not they managed to live a disease-free life is a mystery.

32. The Royal Regurgitation

Regurgitation is the act of vomiting swallowed food. Many animals are known to indulge in this habit, including frogs, fish, reptiles, and the high-ranking Romans. Eating was the favorite pastime of the Roman Nobles and Emperors. They ate two to three meals (sometimes more) in a single sitting. They ate not to fill their bellies but to cherish the taste of their food. They were the original food connoisseurs.

When they felt full after a meal, they would rush to a nearby latrine, throw up, and come back to the table to eat some more. Today, the place where they vomited has come to be known as the vomitorium. In truth, the vomitorium was a passage in an amphitheater. It had nothing to do with the royal regurgitation.

33. Reusing Urine

The Romans didn't waste their urine. They didn't recycle it either. They simply reused it for a variety of purposes. It is rumored that the urine trade was a thriving business in Ancient Rome. This is how it probably came about. Their sewage system wasn't really top-class. The public toilets often overflowed. It was then that the Roman scientists and engineers came up with a unique plan. They started promoting the function and capabilities of the liquid.

Collecting the excess urine from the latrines, they gave it back to the people, claiming that it had a number of useful properties. The dry cleaners used it for cleaning the laundry owing to the alkali component (ammonia) present in it. Over time, it was also used in the production of toothpaste. It is a proven scientific fact that ammonia cleans teeth as well. Apart from using urine-infused toothpaste, Roman dentists applied urine to the teeth to relieve toothache. It was surprisingly effective, though not exactly elegant.

34. Prostitutes Made a Fashion Statement

Prostitution was legal in the Roman Empire, but prostitutes were looked down upon, not just by the nobility but by the commoners, too. Many men (and women) may have engaged their services, but nobody saw them as equals. To differentiate them from other women, they were forced to dye their hair blonde. The Romans were brunettes or black-haired by birth. The barbarians (any foreigners, more specifically Germans, Gauls, and Slavic natives) were blonde. It was the Roman way of insulting both the barbarians and the prostitutes.

However, as time passed, Roman women began liking blonde hair, and many dyed their hair blonde too. There was a sudden influx of blondes on the streets of Rome, and the men were at a complete loss. They didn't know whether to court them or to pay them for their company.

35. Why Was Purple Banned?

The Roman obsession with color differentiation didn't end with hair colors. The color of their clothing mattered a great deal, in particular, the color purple. The common folk and the low-ranking nobles weren't allowed to wear anything with purple in it. This color was reserved only for the emperors and the high-ranking officers in their retinue. Anyone else wandering the streets sporting purple was either incarcerated or punished.

Unlike many of the nonsensical obsessions of the Romans, there was a logical reason behind holding purple in such high regard. Back then, purple was a rare and valuable commodity. It was extracted from snails. To dye a small handkerchief purple, thousands of snails had to be smashed. It wasn't even produced locally. The Romans had to import it from Phoenicia (all the way across the Mediterranean), which raised its price further still.

This begs the question: why was purple banned in the first place? Due to its exorbitant prices, the commoners and lower-class nobles wouldn't have been able to afford it anyway.

36. The Slavery of the Sons

Whenever the Romans conquered a region, they took those who opposed them as slaves. It was a common practice back in the day. Most of their slaves were barbarians. The Empire's citizens were generally protected from slavery, except the sons of the Roman fathers. A father was allowed to sell their son as a slave for a set duration. After the duration was up, the slave owner was expected to return the son to his father in the same condition as he was sold.

However, there was a catch. Fathers weren't allowed to sell their sons more than two times. If they did, then the son could emancipate himself from his parents after the third tenure was up. This weird rule was probably in place so that the father could get some compensation for bringing up a child and, at the same time, not profit too much from the venture.

37. Of the Complicated Rules of Adultery

In Ancient Rome, adultery punishments were sexist in nature, mostly in favor of the husband, but sometimes on the side of the wife, too. Husbands had free rein to cheat on their wives. They were allowed to keep as many mistresses as they could handle and bed any number of prostitutes. The complications arose when the wife committed adultery.

If the husband caught her cheating on him, then there was a strict procedure he needed to follow.

1. Lock the wife and her lover in the room.
2. Find witnesses to her infidelity within 20 hours.
3. Assemble factual evidence of her adultery within three days (when the affair started, places where she fooled around, personal details of the lover, and so on).
4. Present it all before the council to get a divorce.

It was a tough ask for the husband. Imagine his mental state as he tried to fish for answers about his wife's affair and her lover's information. Jealousy would have been the best of his emotions. Then again, he must have had his fair share of infidelities (more than fair due to freedom from consequences), so it's hard to feel sorry for the guy.

That procedure wasn't the worst of it, however. If the council didn't grant a divorce to the husband (possibly due to lack of enough evidence), then it would be assumed that he voluntarily pushed his wife into the arms of her lover. Shame in society aside, he would also face jail time or severe punishment after the fact.

The one silver lining for the husband was if his wife committed adultery with a slave or a prostitute. Then, he could kill the lover and move on.

Questions to Reflect on

1. Did Roman doctors really use dreams to diagnose a physical condition?

2. Why did the Romans believe that Christianity was into cannibalism?

3. Why were Roman fathers allowed to slaughter their entire family?

4. What did the Romans use for bathing, if not soap?

5. Why did Roman women's beauty products smell so bad?

Chapter 4: Medieval Madness (500-1500 CE)

It's a known fact that the Medieval Period exhibits numerous stories showcasing unusually cruel punishment and trial methods. Interestingly enough, you'll also learn from other tales that animals were often subject to the same fate when accused of a crime. One of the many tales you'll find in this chapter is how Queen Eleanor's Court of Love is a tale of a peculiar court system dealing with matters of the heart. The subsequent story depicts the mysterious case of the dancing plague that overtook the citizens of Strasburg in the 16th century. Next, you'll read about the unusual ways people in medieval Germany handled divorce, followed by one of the most bizarre beauty trends of the Middle Ages. You'll also learn how court jesters got away with insulting nobility and how a pope's mysterious writings made people afraid of black cats. The penultimate story depicts yet another eccentric pope and his bizarre acts over his dead predecessor, while the last one provides an insight into one of the most gruesome details of the Crusades.

Court jesters were able to get away with insulting nobility.
https://commons.wikimedia.org/wiki/File:Jean_Fouquet-_Portrait_of_the_Ferrara_Court_Jester_Gonella.JPG

38. Trial by Ordeal

Before juries started ruling over guilt or innocence in court, it was done through a process called trial by order. This practice originated from the Medieval Period when it existed in two main ways: trial by water and fire. The accused's guilt was determined through God's will and interpreted through a predetermined result. For example, an accused set for a trial by water was typically tossed into a large body of water. If the person floated, it meant they were deemed guilty (instead of just thinking they could swim and keep themselves above water). If they drowned, they were found innocent. In a similar practice, the accused had a rope with a knot tied to them and then thrown into a pool of cold water. If they sank lower than the knot tied on the rope, they were innocent, as this meant that the water embraced them by God's will. They were dragged out before they could drown. And just in the previous case, if they didn't go beneath the knot but started floating, they were guilty and rejected by God. However, those who floated didn't fare much better either. Even if they weren't killed outright, their bodies were often severely mutilated to the point that they died soon after. Another form of trial by water involved tossing the accused into boiling water. If they were burned to death, they were innocent. If they survived, they were guilty. Trial by fire was just as gruesome. It involved giving a sizzling hot iron bar for the accused to carry while walking nine feet. Their injuries were then observed to determine whether they cleared up. If the injuries started to heal within three days, the person was deemed innocent. If their wounds began festering (which was common as the lack of hygiene was the perfect breeding ground for infections), they were guilty.

In all forms of trial by ordeal, the interpretation of the result varied, and it was left to the community's discretion. For example, in the trial by hot iron, the judgment of how the persons would be healed depended on the community's opinion on what they considered a clean wound. Likewise, in the rope trial by water, people often didn't simply sink or float but were moving around, trying to avoid drowning. This made determining how low they sank incredibly challenging, so it was up to the onlookers to decide whether the accused went low enough.

Sometimes, they would already know the person had committed the crime, but they lacked proof, while other times, they just wanted someone to be punished for something. False accusations were frequent as well. For example, one story describes how a man visiting his neighbor who owed him money met a gruesome fate at a trial by ordeal. Arriving at his neighbor's house, he did not find anyone home, but he entered to look around, hoping to find something he could ask the neighbor to give him instead of money. When the neighbor arrived home soon after, they immediately accused him of trying to steal - wittily omitting the fact they owed him and escaping the burden of having to pay back. The man was arrested, put to trial by water, and unfortunately for him, he floated.

39. Eleanor of Aquitaine's Court of Love

According to Andreas Capellanus, author and royal chaplain, the Court of Love was a unique trial system run by Queen Eleanor of Aquitaine and her daughter Marie, Countess of Champagne. Some sources claim that it was Marie's idea. Still, she was only able to execute it because of her mother's influence. In contrast, others attribute this unusual court system central to Queen Eleanor. Between 1168 and 1173, the mother-daughter duo held regular hearings, along with Poitier's noblewomen, who acted as judges and juries. However, this court dealt with the most unusual matters, like love and lovers' disagreements. While in Medieval times, people adhered to strict behavioral conduct when it came to courting and relationships, disagreements still arose and needed to be addressed.

With two failed marriages behind her (one to Louis VII of France, the other to Henry, Duke of Normandy) and rumored to be in love with her uncle Raymond, Eleanor was more than equipped to provide an insight into marital and lover's disagreements. However, the true reason behind her court might be forever hidden in mystery. Some sources claim that Eleanor's Court of Love was a social experiment that allowed her to see how people resolved the problems she never caught in her own life. After all, she was active in many other areas of the political scene, the matriarch of their family, and had plenty to do with her time (unlike the noblewomen who used it as a distraction from their boring lives).

40. The Dancing Plague of 1518

In 1518, a woman named Frau Troffea stopped into the July heat in Strasbourg and started dancing as if celebrating something. Except she wasn't; she just started dancing without reason and couldn't stop. She danced until she fainted from exhaustion. After coming to herself, she immediately continued dancing. And soon, she wasn't the only one. In the following week, others around her began dancing as well, and just like Frau Troffea, they didn't stop until they dropped from exhaustion or injury. Alarmed by this unusual phenomenon, authorities quickly started working on the solution. At first, they thought helping those afflicted by providing instructions from professional dancers, music, and guidance on where they could dance would enable them to dance out whatever the cause was. This was mainly because religious leaders thought that the dancers were possessed by demons - they thought the demons would leave if the people exhausted themselves enough. However, this only caused more people to get afflicted - until around 400 people were dancing. Many died from exhaustion, heatstroke, and dehydration, while the rest finally found respite in early September. While historians claim that the dancing plague of Strasbourg was only one of many that occurred throughout history, a conclusive explanation behind this and any other dancing frenzy is yet to be found. Contemporary research theorizes that the people might have been having convulsions (which made them look like they were dancing) after eating rye flour contaminated with ergot, a fungal infection. American medical historian John Waller theorized that the dancing plague was a result of a mass psychogenic disorder brought on by extreme stress. Around that time, people in Strasbourg had to deal with avoiding highly contagious diseases like syphilis and smallpox, not to mention enduring several famines in a row. All these stressors combined could have easily explained this disorder.

41. Animal Trials

As if the uncommonly gruesome trial methods people had to undergo weren't enough, they weren't the only ones who could end up in front of a judge and jury in medieval times. Animals were often publicly accused of crimes and had their trial and verdicts. Pigs were particularly frequently tried (and usually executed), which was not surprising given they often ran wild on the streets instead of being contained like they are nowadays on farms. The most common victims of pig attacks were small children, as they were easy prey and within reach of the omnivore pigs. According to a story depicting the trial of several pigs in September 1379, their crimes went as far as killing people. This story claims that while only a few pigs attacked and killed a man near a French monastery, the other pigs from the same herd (that were peacefully grazing around) were put to trial, too. It was customary for "onlookers" to be tried as well because they were thought to "approve" the crime by not doing anything. All pigs were promptly sentenced to death, but after the Friars from the monastery pleaded on the "onlookers" behalf, these pigs were released. Besides pigs, horses, bulls, eels, sheep, dogs, and even dolphins were among the animals that were commonly tried and found guilty.

While large and easily captured animals were typically sentenced to death, pests and insects had different punishments. People resorted to very unusual methods on this front - from praying insects away to sending letters to rats to vacate their dwellings and leave town. Sometimes, these small animals were even given a specific date by which they had to move on.

Other times, animals were put in jail, along with people, suffering the same fate. And just like with people, sometimes innocent animals were tried and sentenced too. In the late 16th century, naturalist Leonhard

Thurneysser brought a moose into a small Swiss town. Having not seen this animal before, the locals feared it and considered it a vicious beast even though they hadn't even dared to approach it. In just a short time, they tried and sentenced it to death. According to another story, a mule was executed along with a man presumed to be its owner (they were even sure of this - they just found the animal beside the man), who was found guilty of robbery.

Fortunately, by the late 16th century, animals started to get their defenders. Sometimes, these were people who relied on animals for labor and sustenance and didn't want to lose them. Other times, the defenders were like Bartholomew Chassenée, who gained fame after successfully defending rats against the accusation they ate and destroyed a good amount of barley in Autun in France. Chassenée's arguments were clever indeed. He claimed that rats couldn't have committed the crime, nor could they be summoned to the court because they were watched all the time by cats! Chassenée later defended insects just as successfully. These creatures were tried by an ecclesiastical court, which threatened to bring an anathema (a form of excommunication for animals) upon them. This was a common yet ineffective way of punishing insects and other pests. For example, when weevils plagued St. Julien in the 16th century, they were excommunicated through public prayers. While the insects migrated away (probably because they found a better place to live rather than due to the prayers), they returned three decades later. This time, the weevils were put to trial, but they had a great defender who argued that they, like people, were God's creations, and he placed them on Earth and with the sustenance they had (crops) for a reason. The prosecution, in turn, argued that as animals, weevils should be people's subordinates, which meant they shouldn't eat crops meant for people. People of St. Julien proposed a compromise, setting up a place where weevils could stand and feed near the town. However, the defense rejected this, arguing the place didn't have enough sustenance for the weevils. The trial lasted eight long months, but the verdict remains a mystery because the court documents containing it were destroyed (perhaps by the weevils themselves.)

42. Divorce by Physical Combat

Given their German Celtic origins, it's not surprising that people in Medieval Germany resolved disputes with combat. The Germanic law at the time allowed for a trial by combat, which allowed the disputants to resolve issues by legal duels. This was usually the case when the parties couldn't present any other form of evidence (like witnesses or confessions) to prove their case. However, trial by combat was also applied in unusual situations, like divorce.

According to Hans Talhoffer's Fechtbuch (published in 1467), which contains a faithful depiction of duels at the time, these trials had specific rules. For example, since men had the advantage of being trained for combat, they were to stand in a three-foot hole, while women could move freely around them. Likewise, men were given normal-sized swinging clubs, while women were armed with rocks and wrapped a cloth a little longer than the men's club to match each other's swinging range. They both wore a simple unitard with stirrup legs, the most practical clothes at the time. Usually, each had three clubs/rocks. If the women attacked the men when those were in a vulnerable position (picking or putting down their clubs), they had to give up one of their rocks. If men touched the outer edge of their hole (which was seen as an attempt to get out of the hole), they, too, had to hand over one of their clubs. Despite these clear instructions, declaring a victor in these situations was tricky. While the book mentioned above only describes fighting until one party loses their weapons or is physically unable to continue (which was often, as they were attacking each other with blunt objects), others believe that judges decided when to put an end to these trials. According to yet another theory, the men could win if they managed to pull the women into the hole, while women won if they dragged the men out of the hole. The only clarity provided through history was that whoever won the battle won the dispute, too. In divorce trials, this meant that if the party who proposed the divorce won, they could separate from their spouse. If the winner was the spouse who didn't want the divorce, the couple had to remain together.

43. Hairless Beauties

Beauty trends come and go, and history has seen some strange practices and habits. However, the Middle Ages were riddled with the most bizarre trends - and the reasons behind them were even more baffling. Unlike modern women who place much emphasis on growing thick and healthy-looking eyelashes and eyebrows, in the Middle Ages, less was more. Women who weren't gifted with fair, thin, and barely visible facial hair would pluck everything out just to achieve that beautiful bald look. Not only that, but at one time, the oval face was all the rage, forcing women to "reshape" their face by plucking their hairline too. The higher the hairline went, the better, to the extent that some women decidedly resembled middle-aged, balding men rather than being the ladies they were. Removing eyelashes and eyebrows further accentuated the bald forehead and was seen as a sign of wealth and status, as only the nobility had time to spend their days plucking their hair.

44. How Being Funny Paid Off in the Medieval Court

The lords and ladies of the Medieval court were highly respected members of the society, and those disrespecting them met a gruesome faith. From corporal punishment to death, the sentences for offending court members varied by offense and country. Even those who were only suspected of committing this offense suffered the same and were rarely given the chance to prove their innocence. One group of people was exempt from this rule - the court jesters. They might have had one of the worst "work uniforms" in history (given they wore hats shaped like donkey's ears), but court jesters had numerous privileges. They could speak freely about whatever they wanted, as most of what they said was seen as just one of their "jokes." Taking advantage of this freedom - and their ability to weave the most creative insults into their performance - they often shared their dissatisfaction with court members and forbidden political views. Not only could they get away with it, but they also got paid handsomely.

45. How Black Cats Got Condemned

Not surprisingly, even the fear-mongering surrounding black cats stems from the Middle Ages. It all started with Pope Gregory IX's unusual publication in 1232. Named Vox in Rama, this document detailed the practices of witches living in northern Germany. While it's unclear how Gregory learned of these rituals, he described them in great detail, exploring each secret of these cults. For example, he revealed the spells the witches used to call on the Devil himself. He wrote about an unusual secret ingredient they need to complete these and many other spells - to kiss a black cat. Gregory claimed that witches adored black cats, starting the rumor that these animals are associated with dark magic. Soon, tales of black cats being used in rituals of the Cathars and the Waldenses emerged, and cats became hunted animals. Just like inquisitors were sent by the Church to capture the heretics, cat hunters were hired to eradicate all the feline population. To do a thorough job and avoid black cats popping up in the future, the hunters reduced the entire cat population in Rome to near-extinction levels. Ironically, the severe lack of cats led to the overpopulation of rats in the city, which played a massive role in the outbreak of several diseases that later decimated the city's human population, including The Plague.

46. The Bizarre Trial of Pope Formosus

Pope Formosus was put on trial for being a pope by his successor.
Municipal Library of Trento, CC0, via Wikimedia Commons:
https://commons.wikimedia.org/wiki/File:Formosus,_Papa_Formoso.jpg

Pope Formosus had the misfortune of being put on trial for being a pope by his successor in 897. What made this already unusual circumstance even more peculiar was that Formosus was already dead for almost a year at the time of his trial. Nevertheless, his successor, Pope Stephen VI, had his body dug up and brought to the Basilica San Giovanni Laterano in Rome. Here, Stephen VI brought up several charges against Formosus, made numerous heated arguments, and finally convicted the already dead man, giving a bizarre sentence consisting of several parts. First, Formosus' papal clothes were removed from his body, and his fingers were cut off. Then, he was reburied, dug up again, and tossed in the Tiber. Soon after, Formosus' supporters started a rumor that his body was washed up to the shores, was resurrected, and started granting miracles. They also turned against Stephen VI, capturing him, throwing him into jail, and ultimately killing him. The Church did nothing to stop them because, by this time, Stephen VI had been excommunicated (stripped of all the spiritual blessings and privileges provided by the Church). Stephen VI has been known to do bizarre things even before and was even rumored to be involved in corruption scandals and other crimes surrounding the Catholic Church (some say this insane trial was his way of trying to deflect from his crimes), and this act was the last drop in the bucket of all that made him unsuitable for the papacy. His successor, Theodore II, overturned the verdict issued against Formosus and banned trials against corpses.

47. Crusades Led By Children

The Crusades, the Catholic Church's holy wars, were one of the darkest moments of the Middle Ages. What's even more bizarre about them is that children often joined willingly and led their troops to the battle. After being denied permission to join the mission by Philip of France, 12-year-old Stephen joined forces with Nicholas, a boy of a similar age, recruiting thousands of children to join the Crusades. Stephen and many other children who joined claimed they received the call from Christ himself and considered their duty to help reclaim the Holy Land. However, most of the children never even reached the battlefields, but they haven't returned home either. Some were victims of a shipwreck after the ship they took toward the Holy Land was caught in a vicious storm. The remaining children made the mistake of boarding ships that took them to Egypt instead, where they were sold as slaves. A few children of Nicholas' groups reached Rome, but it's unclear what happened to them. They, just like the rest of the children who joined the Crusades, were forgotten by the Church and most of the world. Only a few decades ago, when historians researching the Crusades stumbled upon the mention of child soldiers and entire regiments led by children was their devotion and bravery finally acknowledged.

Questions to Reflect on

1. What do you think about the fact that both people and animals had to suffer gruesome trials to prove their innocence in the Middle Ages?

2. Do you think the Court of Love was an effective way to resolve the matters of the heart, or was it just a source of entertainment for the nobility?

3. What's your opinion about the questionable edicts and acts of popes in the Middle Ages?

4. What do you think drove thousands of children to join the bloody wars of the Crusades?

Chapter 5: Renaissance: The Puzzling Practices of the Modern World (1300-1600 CE)

The dawn of the Renaissance marked the beginning of European enlightenment, as the European community took steady steps away from the darkness of the Middle Ages. The French word "Renaissance" translates to "Re-Birth." The Renaissance manifested first in Italy before spreading to the rest of Europe. Fashion and art showed significant leaps in techniques and taste. Artists such as Michelangelo, Rafael, and Leonardo da Vinci were celebrated for their exceptional works and never-before-seen depictions of then-modern life.

Michelangelo was celebrated for his depictions of life during the Renaissance.
https://commons.wikimedia.org/wiki/File:Michelangelo_Daniele_da_Volterra_(dettaglio).jpg

A primary reason for the flourishing of the Renaissance in Italy was due to trade deals that were struck with Eastern Europe and Asia, bringing a lot of wealth into Florence. These riches put quite a few families on the map, including the infamous Medici family. The Medici family used their finances to commission artists for private and public work. The more money they spent on artists, the more freedom the artists had to hone their craft and compete with one another for the money, producing exceptional pieces people are still in awe of today.

Another bittersweet reason for the birth of the Renaissance is the Black Plague. The disease had claimed a lot of souls across Europe. However, as the economy started bouncing back, fewer people fought over employment and riches, raising the societal standard for most of the population.

People started renewing their interest in culture, feverously trying to reeducate themselves in all matters that concerned human civilizations and intellect. With that being said, that era was not without its oddities and out of the extraordinary stories. To say that there were some unusual beliefs among the inhabitants of Europe at the time would be a massive understatement.

48. Blood and Bones

If there are any vampire and zombie enthusiasts out there, gather around!

The Renaissance wasn't only known for its art and culture. During the rebirth era, the practice of drinking human blood and feasting on their bones, fat, and skulls was considered an act to promote one's good health. They would drink fresh human blood, spread human fat onto their bread, and distill human bones into much-coveted spirits. It might sound savage and barbaric, but they believed it all for the sake of healing!

Many were advocating for the health benefits of human blood. Marsilio Ficino, a 15th-century Italian scholar and priest, claimed that if an elderly person wishes to reconnect with their youth again, they should drink the blood of an adolescent. This way, they would regain the vitality of their once young self again.

Blood wasn't only consumed by directly drinking it. They would powder it or create a jam with numerous healing properties. Bones were also coveted to distill. It's been claimed that King Charles II, who had an interest in chemistry and owned a laboratory, was a fan of distilled bones turned into spirits for their health properties. It was so famous that they named it "The King's Drops."

The Art and Artists

The masterpieces of some of the most renowned artists of the Renaissance era have stood the test of time, garnering the admiration of onlookers and easily competing with and surpassing present-day art forms.

Many remarkable works of art paved the way for contemporary artists, including Leonardo da Vinci's Mona Lisa and The Last Supper paintings, The Garden of Earthly Delights by Bosch, Michelangelo's Sistine Chapel ceiling and the David statue, and The Madonna del Prato by Raphael. The intricate details and attention given to every brush stroke in the paintings and every cut chiseled in the stones of their sculptures were a testament to their brilliance and unparalleled artistry.

However, like all things in life, no one is perfect, and even these great names have some peculiar contributions to history that are often overlooked because their artistry overpowers their personal reputations.

49. Leonardo da Vinci

Born as Leonardo di ser Piero da Vinci, he was also known for being a musician and an inventor, not only an artist. He had a long list of innovations, including the parachute and the initial sketch that the modern-day helicopters are believed to be based on. However, many people may not know that the genius did not attend school at all. The young artist was taught how to read, write, and do simple math, but aside from that, he was left to gather the rest of his knowledge on his own and through experience. Quite an impressive feat, given that his achievements have lived centuries after his passing.

His inquisitive mind and interest in all that surrounded him – especially the natural life – influenced many of his life's works, like the behaviors of the birds of prey and water properties. He took an interest in both the human and animal bodies, dissecting and performing autopsies to try to understand what made them tick. He was probably one of the pioneers in mapping the muscles and vascular systems accurately.

On the other hand, his mind also gave way to some questionable eccentricities. The Renaissance man liked to write in reverse. Upon his death, 6000 pages worth of journals were uncovered detailing his inventions, ideas, and, in some cases, grocery lists. However, a lot of those were written backward.

To be able to decipher the writing, the reader would need to hold up the journal to a mirror to understand Leonardo's inner thoughts. While many theorized that this method of documentation was used as a sort of code or cipher, a simpler explanation was presented, which is that he was just trying to avoid smudging the letters together. Leonardo was a lefty; if he had written from left to right, chances are the words would have blended together, given that the ink used at the time didn't dry as quickly. He was just trying to be neat. Another speculated explanation was that he was dyslexic and ambidextrous, which meant he could draw with one hand and write backward with the other.

Upon closer inspection of his journals, an intriguing fact about the inventor was revealed: he was possibly a vegetarian. He was an animal lover and often criticized the morality of consuming them. According to Giorgio Vasari, da Vinci had a habit of purchasing birds for sale just to set them free.

50. Michelangelo Buonarroti

Known best for his artistry in creating the David statue (from a discarded piece of marble) that stands proudly in Florence, Michelangelo's life was not without its interesting twists. Buonarroti had a wide array of talents, including painting, sculpting, architecture, and poetry. It seemed to be the vibe of the era to not centralize yourself in one profession, tossing away any semblance of boredom or routine.

Michelangelo was such a prodigy that he produced two of his masterpieces at the young age of 15, The Madonna of the Stairs and the Battle of the Centaurs.

Most people wouldn't know that the creative mind behind the Sistine Chapel ceiling was openly described as petty, short-tempered, and had no shortage of rivals. Also, he sort of started his career with forgery.

At the beginning of his career, the artist was commissioned by Lorenzo de' Medici to create a sculpture of a Greek-style cupid. Medici then suggested to Buonarroti to bury the statue in the sand, giving it an air of authenticity so it would be sold for a higher price. After agreeing to the scheme and digging out the statue they buried, it was sold for a substantial amount of money to Cardinal Raffaele Riario. Shortly after the deception, the Cardinal was able to identify the statue as a replica and got his money back. Ironically, though, the work on the statue was so detailed and beautiful that he was impressed enough to invite Michelangelo to a meeting in Rome and commission him to create the Pieta, essentially launching his artistic career.

Michelangelo's rivalries were many. One of them ended with him having a broken nose that remained disfigured for the rest of his life. Young Pietro Torrigiano was said to have been provoked by condescending remarks from Michelangelo that he punched him in the face, crushing his nose. Torrigiano described the incident by saying, "I delivered him such a hard knock on the nose that I felt bone and cartilage crumble beneath my knuckles like a biscuit, and he'll carry this mark with him to the grave."

Jealousy played a huge part in his rivalry with another well-known artist, Raphael. In an effort to put an end to Michelangelo's career, Raphael convinced Pope Julius to hire the former to paint the Sistine Chapel, believing that the huge commission would surely be too overwhelming for Buonarroti and that when it came to the art of painting, he was the superior choice. This belief came from Michelangelo's reputation at the time for being an exceptional sculptor with not much painting experience. Reluctant at first, he eventually accepted the commission and spent four long years lying on scaffolding, painting the ceiling, producing one of the modern world's most admired masterpieces to this day. He added a little Easter egg in the work, by painting his likeness into the ceiling as Saint Bartholomew.

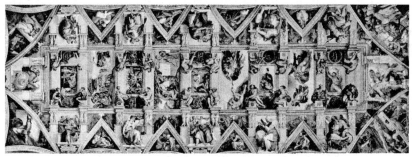

Michelangelo painted the ceiling of the Sistine Chapel.

Another interesting rivalry that ended with petty revenge from the artist occurred during his work on The Last Judgment painting. He was visited by Pope Paul III with the pope's entourage, and among them was Biagio da Cesena, the master of ceremonies. Biagio foolishly didn't shy away from giving his opinion on Buonarroti's work. He was disgusted by the amount of naked figures displayed in the art, stating that it was only fit to hang in a bar. Little did he know, those condescending words would not go unpunished by the artist. In retribution, Michelangelo painted Biagio as the judge of the souls in hell, Minos. This may not seem like such a harsh payback until the onlooker realizes he painted him surrounded by serpents who were actively trying to bite off his private parts.

Michelangelo wasn't particularly fond of personal hygiene. The man hated to bathe with a vengeance. He also didn't change his clothes very often, so much so that when he died, his garments had to be peeled off and cut away from his body.

He was also commissioned by nine popes for several works of art and continued to work until the very week of his death. Even though he couldn't physically move, he still instructed others from afar. He died at the age of 88, a much longer span of life than what was common during that time.

51. Hieronymus Bosch

Bosch was born in the Netherlands into a family of painters. Johannes Thomas Zoon van Aken (whose name is quite the mouthful), his grandfather, was a renowned painter in the first half of the 15th century. Bosch's name may not ring as loud as Michelangelo's or da Vinci's; nonetheless, he is considered a revolutionary and may have shaped the face of contemporary art as it is known today.

He was heavily influenced by his religious background, something he carried with him in the depictions of his paintings. His imagination played a significant role in his art. Not only did he include Christian references, such as heaven and hell, but he also had a habit of making up monstrous and wondrous creatures, incorporating them into his work. He made up his own interpretations from the Bible and preferred to use his own vision when presenting them rather than gathering inspiration from the works of art made by painters in the past. This approach earned him the title "Painter of Dreams."

His paintings were a beautiful blend of holiness and idiosyncrasy. His art was usually quite big, it had to be divided into triptychs (a three-part painting). The most famous of them all is "The Garden of Earthly Delights."

The triptych was no ordinary painting of a party; it was an artistic vision documenting the wedding of Count Henry II of Nassau's daughter. Bosch wanted to capture the "benefits and hazards" of being married on his canvas. On the left-hand side, Adam and Eve are depicted in Eden. In the center, a hedonistic paradise is displayed, and on the far right, with a panel of blazing hell that awaits the sinners. Needless to say, his ideas on marriage may have been a bit extreme. Bosch was far from done. On the outer frame of the painting, he drew the origin or the birth of the world. Specifically the third day of creation, when the "earthly paradise" was formed in grayish colors. In the upper left corner was his rendition of God holding an open book with the Latin inscription, "For he spoke, and it came to be; he commanded, and it stood firm."

Bosch's imagination ran wild with this painting. In the left panel, he drew another youthful God officiating the marriage of Adam and Eve. The area around them was filled with animals, trees, and mythical creatures, with a magnificent structure floating on a lake. The middle panel was populated as well with Bosch's incredible creatures, illustrating the development of The Garden of Eden. Bosch chose to keep the figures nude to indicate that this was prior to humanity's expulsion from heaven. He did include a lot of references to sin, though in the form of strawberries and musical instruments, foreseeing humanity's eventual descent into hell and damnation. On the right panel, the musical instruments are seen and interpreted as tools of torture. It is believed that the painting may have included a self-portrait of himself in the center as the tree man, a mere observer of the scene, much like the artist himself.

Without a doubt, Bosch had quite a dark sense of humor when he chose this chaotic and magnificent piece to give to the newlyweds.

The Bone Churches

One specific oddity, and perhaps the oddest thing about it, was that it was considered normal during the Renaissance churches adorned with human bones and skulls. These churches and chapels were everywhere, a lot of them still standing today.

52. The Kutna Hora Church of Bones

A known sight in the Czech Republic, the Sedlec Ossuary is a spectacle coupled with quite an unusual story behind it.

This place gives a new meaning to the statement "built with blood and sweat," except there are bones too. The church is a statement that art can be performed by humans and with humans.

Tens of thousands of people were buried in that church's cemetery. The lower levels of the church were meant to house the bones laid to rest. This was before the incredible idea of turning dead human bones into pieces of décor came about. As legend would state, the idea was proposed by a half-blind monk.

The Sedlec Ossuary is in the small city of Kutna Hora. As visitors enter it, they will see bones on the walls, bones hanging from the ceiling, chandelier bones, and large cases displaying bones. Femurs, tibias, and pyramids of skulls cover almost every surface the eye can see.

The story goes something like this: in 1278, a priest made his way back from Jerusalem with a jar of "holy soil." The soil was scattered in the area, making it a favorable spot for burials. Two things happened over the following century: the Black Death hit Europe and the Hussite wars. The body count was enormous, to the extent that there was no room to bury more people in that area since the holy soil made it more popular than other places to dispose of the dead.

A new Cemetery, Church of All Saints, was built around 1400, which led to some of the bodies being dug up and their bones placed beneath the church in storage.

Another century passed, and it was decided that all bodies should be dug up and stored in the Ossuary as well for safekeeping.

So, who decided to create the masterpieces of bones? Well, it is believed that the half-blind monk arranged the initial bones and skulls into pyramid shapes, and this fantastical act returned his vision back to him.

The rest of the artistic display of bones was made by a wood carver called Frantisek Rint. Why did someone think this was a good idea? And who made the decision to display them like that remains a mystery. However, in the minds of the artists and decision-makers, this act was to honor the dead.

53. Santuario di San Bernardino alle Ossa

In the year 1142, a hospital and cemetery were built in Milan, Italy. It took the doctors 702 more years to realize that they needed to wash their hands. Subsequently, by 1210, there was no more space to bury the dead in the graveyard. A solution to the predicament was presented by building a tiny ossuary chapel to keep the bones of the dead in it. In 1269, a church was erected by the ossuary. In 1679, Giovanni Andrea Biffi renovated the structure and, in the process, decided to use the human bones stored in the ossuary as pieces of décor, specifically using skulls and tibias.

It's a bit confusing for the public to find the location of the church, as there are two built side by side. One is adorned with human bones, and one is with a priest who leads masses with a guitar, so they sort of have a yin and yang situation going on.

54. The Catacombs of Paris

Paris is one of the biggest cities in the world that houses ossuaries filled with human bones, specifically six million dead bodies. These catacombs easily date back to Roman times.

On a rainy day in the spring of 1780, the Cimetiere des Saints looked like a scene from The Walking Dead due to the overflowing bodies. By September, no more bodies were allowed to be buried in Les Innocents or any other Paris cemetery. The bodies were unearthed, and the bones were moved to the catacombs.

At the start of the moving process, the catacombs were filled with unorganized piles of discarded bones. In 1810, Louis-Etienne Hericart de Thury made the executive decision to transform the chaos into a visitable museum. Louis had a bit of a dramatic bone in him. He liked to stack the femurs and skulls in morbid and disturbing patterns, with decorations and signs that read, "Stop, this is the empire of death." He also made a special room displaying the skeletal deformities in the catacombs.

Some factions may see this as a tasteless display of the dead, but not all people share this sentiment. In 2004, the Parisian police found a movie theater complete with a large screen, seats, and projector, a bar, and a restaurant within one of the caverns.

55. The Automata of the Renaissance

Some people believe that the dawn of automation, robotics, and interest in all things mechanical only started in the most recent century. They couldn't be more wrong.

In the 15th century, a genuine interest in automata started to brew, with various works of art, devices, and inventions developed at the hands of some of the most renowned inventors like Leonardo da Vinci.

French philosopher and mathematician Rene Descartes is credited with raising the interest of the world in the field. He theorized that the anatomy of animals was no more complicated than machines and that they could easily be replicated using mechanical tools.

Wondrous contraptions were created by the hands of the German inventor Johannes Müller von Königsberg, including a mechanical eagle and the astounding wooden bird that he managed to make fly from Konigsberg (Nuremberg) to greet and salute Emperor Maximilian and return back.

Leonardo da Vinci's mechanical Lion was also quite impressive, created in honor of Louis XII, the contraption could wag its tail, open its mouth, and stand up on its hind legs.

A 16th-century clockwork monk can be found in the Smithsonian. The mechanical man is accredited to Juanelo Turriano. The little device can move his head, mouth, and limbs, beat his chest, and roll his eyes. All of this was made possible with a key-wound spring wholly hidden inside the body of the small monk.

Questions to Reflect on

1. How do you think the belief that ingesting bones and blood promoted health came about? What was the trigger, and who dared to try it first and encourage it?
2. Had the families of the dead been alive at the time that the bones were dug up and used for church decorations, do you believe they would have been flattered or appalled at the use of their loved one's remains?
3. What do you think Bosch's mythical creatures represented, and what inspired them? Could it be that he truly is the painter of dreams, simply putting on the canvas what he saw in his sleep?

4. Do you think Michelangelo's ego was justified, or was his talent easily surpassed by other artists of his time?

Chapter 6: The Enlightenment: Bizarre Breakthroughs (1600-1800 CE)

Although a period categorized by its intellectual advances, the Enlightenment was a period of equal amounts of interesting, unusual, and downright weird tales. Starting with the stories of the Great Moon Hoax and Mesmerism, this chapter reflects on some of the most outlandish claims made during this period. The story of the decapitated frog legs and the one about cows' role in vaccine development are both unusual but still depict incredibly significant scientific discoveries. Galileo's confirmation of the Copernican system and Newton's Explains gravity are likewise the foundation for modern scientific theories, although their significance also lies in the fact they went against what people knew and accepted at the time. The same applies to the ideas of Voltaire, Hobbes, and Locke, which, as described in the two subsequent stories, helped shape the foundation of modern society and political beliefs. The last two stories depict how the microscope was discovered and how a new, much more useful device, like an air pump, served as a bizarre form of entertainment during the Enlightenment.

56. The Folly of the Great Moon Hoax

In 1835, New York City's daily newspaper, The Sun, started publishing a series of articles describing the research of John Herschel, a renowned astronomer and the son of William Herschel, whose name is tied to the discovery of Uranus. The first of the six installments of this series started with the younger Herschel building an enormous telescope to study the planetary bodies. It then goes on to describe how Herschel used this device to correct and solve many mathematical problems astronomers at the time encountered. However, the most puzzling claim the articles made was that Herschel discovered veritable proof of life on the Moon. Now, this life wasn't in the form of fossils or frozen water like scientists would expect to find. The articles describe Herschel's finding as the biggest clue that solved this mystery, which became known as the Great Moon Hoax. Looking through his telescope, Herschel purportedly saw unusual birds with somewhat humanlike forms, long-beaked cranes, goat-like creatures dancing around playfully, miniature bison, and many other life forms one would expect to see in a science fiction movie or book.

John Herschel was said to have discovered life on the moon.
https://commons.wikimedia.org/wiki/File:Sir_John_Frederick_William_Herschel._Mezzotint_by_W._Ward,_1_Wellcome_V0002717_(cropped)-34-(brightness).jpg

As later turned out, the great discovery never happened and wasn't authorized by John Herschel either. The articles were the result of British writer Richard Adams Locke's vivid imagination and incredible writing skills who, after arriving to work at the Sun, looked for a way to boost sales. Locke claimed he never thought so many people would believe the story. He intended to create a satirical series that parodies the works of amateur astronomers who made similarly outlandish claims during their "research." While initially intending to clarify the truth behind the stories right away, the sheer amount of sales they generated stopped Locke from doing so. Not only did some people believe them, but some religious congregations even started organizing missionary expeditions to work on the Moon. One person who discredited the stories was the writer Edgar Allan Poe. While acknowledging that even scientists claimed that finding life on the Moon was possible and being thoroughly impressed by Locke's writing skills, Poe didn't want to give it credit because he believed it resembled too much a story of his own!

57. Mesmerism and the World of Animal Magnetism

Animal magnetism, also known as Mesmerism, was an 18th-century healing method relying on harmony with nature and its forces invisible to the naked eye. It was invented by German physician Franz Anton Mesmer, who claimed to use the powers of a universal magnetic fluid to heal and restore. According to Mesmer, this fluid was found in all living beings and affected them equally. By manipulating this fluid within a body with magnets, he could restore the balance to the body and cure any disease.

Mesmer experimented with this method in Paris, where he claimed to have success in both creating and relieving pain in people without touching them. By simply manipulating people's fluid with magnets, he could affect them from a distance or even through the walls. He presented it as a form of mass treatment for any disease or condition. As Paris was the city quick to follow scientific advancement and modern trends during the Enlightenment, Mesmerism quickly won the masses' approval. However, when Mesmer tried to gain validation from the Faculty of Medicine, the Royal Society of Medicine, and the Royal Academy of Sciences, he hit a brick wall. Not only were these institutions unconvinced of Mesmer's claims, but King Louis XVI established the Royal Commission specifically to investigate the science behind them. As expected, the commission members had a hard time proving that this mysterious fluid even existed. They didn't know where to look for it, how to access it, or how to measure its properties. According to Mesmer, the fluid could be detected only by the senses of the being through which it courses, and an outsider could observe it only by looking at its effect on living beings. For all these reasons, the commission decided that Mesmerism's true effect lay in the power of suggestion and not in valid scientific reasoning. The commission outlined the fact that people who believed to be under the effect of Mesmerism were visibly in a trance-like state. Moreover, people often claimed to feel the healing effects of distant animal magnetism even when nothing was sent their way. Accepting these as just examples of the expectations and imagination of the subjects, the Royal Commission effectively dismissed animal magnets as a valid treatment method.

58. The Decapitated Frog Legs

In a groundbreaking experiment in 1786, Italian physicist and physician Luigi Galvani lined several dead frogs, attaching them by their spines with a metal hook. To his surprise, as they were dangling, one of the hooks accidentally made contact with an iron plate that had electricity running through it, and the frog's legs started twitching. While he was already conducting experiments on muscle motion on dissected animals, the discovery that they can be sparked to life with electricity was just a serendipitous coincidence. Blurring the lives between life and death in the public imagination, Galvani began to publicly boast about his discovery, describing how the spasms and contractions of frog legs occurred. Soon, other scientists started similar experiments, although they didn't limit themselves to mere frog legs anymore. They used other, larger animals whose bodies made the effect even more shocking. Some even experimented on human bodies (dead and alive), investigating whether this was a vital force that fostered life in living beings. Galvani named this phenomenon animal electricity, but it was renamed galvanism to honor his discovery.

59. From Cows to Humans

Infectious diseases have been plaguing humanity since the beginning of time. While researching smallpox, English physician Edward Jenner stumbled upon a fortuitous discovery. Being a highly infectious condition, smallpox often affects entire families and communities. However, Jenner noticed that not everyone who was around smallpox patients fell ill themselves. When asking the family members of smallpox victims about their medical history, Jenner discovered that those who didn't catch smallpox had suffered from cowpox before. Led by a strong belief that these people were immunized against smallpox. He inoculated several healthy people with material from cowpox pustules and, after waiting for the inoculation period to be over, infected them with smallpox. Since the candidates did not develop this disease, Jenner proved his theory and the effectiveness of inoculation with small amounts of biological material of the pathogen behind the infection.

60. Galileo Confirming the Copernican System

As a pioneer of the Scientific Revolution, Galileo Galilei entered the history books to prove the heliocentric system, confirming that the Earth (just like every other planetary body) moves around the Sun. The idea of the Sun being the center of the universe wasn't anything new. It was first developed by Polish astronomer Nicolaus Copernicus during the 16th century. It all began when Copernicus stumbled upon an Ancient Greek belief claiming that the Sun represents the center and the driving force behind the Universe.

Galileo confirmed the Copernicus theory.
https://commons.wikimedia.org/wiki/File:Galileo.arp.300pix.jpg

After studying the movement of different planets across the sky for 25 years, Copernicus came to the same conclusion. However, given that this went against the religious beliefs most scholars operated under at the time, Copernicus knew that his theory would be rejected. As much as it was backed by common sense, it had no better explanation as to why the planets move the way they did than the notion their movements were governed by God, who created the Earth. Although the views were still similar when Galileo began to argue for this theory, things were about to change. Unlike Copernicus, Galileo had access to telescopes (he built them after a model devised by Dutch lens makers who also invented microscopes) and mathematical data collected by Tycho Branch, the scientist who also took an interest in the Copernican theory. Besides discovering four moons orbiting around Jupiter and that the Earth's moon had an uneven surface, Galileo also observed that the planetary motions support the heliocentric theory (as opposed to the widely accepted geocentric one).

These controversial findings led to conflict with the Church because they went against its authority and teachings. Fearing that if people started to believe in theories like this, they would start questioning other religious teachings too, Church authorities warned Galileo to stop spreading Copernicus's ideas. Despite this, in 1632, he published the "*Dialogue Concerning the Two Chief World Systems*," which outlined the same ideas. This public display of support for Copernican theory landed Galileo in a trial before the Inquisition. Despite agreeing to publicly retract his support of the heliocentric theory, Galileo remained a prisoner in his own home near Florence. Still trying to stubbornly retain some of his rights to believe in the Sun being the center of the Universe, Galileo stared into it day after day from sun-up to sundown until he went blind. Over time, scientists started to steer away from traditional beliefs and take new approaches to scientific methodology. Due to this intense separation of science and religion, Galileo's confirmation of the Copernican system became accepted as well.

61. Newton Explains the Law of Gravity

In an era where people lived with the belief that all forces on the Earth and the Universe were controlled by God, Isaac Newton's theory of gravity was a shocking and somewhat unwelcome revelation. However, Newton was prepared to explain how gravitational forces worked and how they caused every object to be affected by them equally. He pulled out numerous mathematical principles established by scientists many years ago.

As he explained in his book, *"The Mathematical Principles of Natural Philosophy,"* published in 1687, he came to this conclusion when he discovered that the same forces controlled the movement of the planetary bodies as they did everything on Earth. Newton's law of gravitation explained that every object attracts another, describing the entire Universe as a massive clock. He could also prove mathematically how all parts of this clock worked together. However, to avoid being completely condemned for his radical ideas, Newton also added that while God didn't control this mechanism, he created it. Unfortunately, the latter claim made fellow scientists hesitant to consider his ideas for a short time. However, soon came the time that people became divided on scientific beliefs. After all, plenty of scientists were ready to embrace combined ideas that weren't as radical as some of the other scientific discoveries at the time, nor were sticking rigidly to traditional beliefs - but represented a middle ground they could embrace.

62. Voltaire's Fight against Intolerance

As the Enlightenment progressed, fake news similar to the Moon Hoax became almost an everyday occurrence, much to the annoyance of those who wished to entertain only progressive ideas that would contribute to the benefit of all. One of these was François Marie Arouet, better known as Voltaire. Voltaire had very good reasons to use a pen name instead of his own. Across his 70+ publications, he often targeted the government, the aristocracy, the religious leaders, and pretty much everyone who used the public to create a sensation - whether to deflect from their misdeeds or to promote something that only benefited them.

After fake news about a Lisbon earthquake, which was nothing but sensationalism in newspapers, making a fortune for its owners, Voltaire started an even harsher controversy. Enveloped in satire, his sharp opinions got him in trouble with the authorities. However, being the brilliant thinker he was, he negotiated his exile to England, where he continued his radical battle against intolerance and even branched out to embrace freedom of speech and religious beliefs. He claimed that even when he disagreed with someone else's ideas, he readily helped them defend their right to express them. While social justice warriors like these are common in modern times, during the Enlightenment, people were happy to encounter one who was as fervent in their stance as Voltaire. His radical ideas made him numerous powerful enemies, but he persisted.

Eventually, he and other thinkers and writers who used their quills as weapons against injustice made the breakthrough they were waiting for. People were awakened to see the benefits of life without prejudice, intolerance towards others' beliefs, and superstition based on age-old religious ideas without substance.

63. Hobbes and Locke: Social Contracts and Natural Rights

Scientists weren't the only ones who encountered unusual breakthroughs during the Enlightenment. Some of the period's greatest thinkers expressed their ideas in never-before-seen ways, which only elevated the shock factor with their innovative ideas. Thomas Hobbes, for example, made a quote after publishing his work *"Leviathan"* or *"The Matter, Forme and Power of a Commonwealth Ecclesiasticall and Civil"* in 1651. Being thoroughly disappointed with human selfishness and wickedness after the English Civil War, Hobbs came to the idea that people needed strong leadership so they could stop fighting against each other. He saw the solution in people giving their rights to their ruler, who, in turn, gave them order and law. This alone was a far cry from the practice of having numerous rulers, which both religious and civil people were accustomed to for centuries. According to Hobbes, the leader needed absolute authority, comparing the power he would give the ruler to that of the mythical Leviathan, the sea monster - effectively shocking the religious leaders with his idea. This absolute power could impose order but provide stability and safety in return, creating what Hobbes called a Social Contract.

Another Enlightenment thinker, John Locke, had a more optimistic outlook, claiming that people are born good and they just turn away from their positive values due to bad experiences. However, when given a chance, they could relearn them and improve their behavior and disposition. Locke was against absolute monarchy and argued for letting people govern themselves as he believed this to be the natural order. He theorized that people could govern their lives and the lives of their society because they were born with certain natural rights. People's right to life, property, and liberty allowed them to act freely, and according to Locke, it was the government's job to ensure they would be able to do this. He believed that the government should have limited influence and could be overthrown by the people if necessary. Needless to say, this was another radical idea that went against the previously circulating political views, not to mention the wishes of current religious and civil leaders.

Despite the authorities' attempts to oppress them, Locke's and Hobbes's ideas had a monumental impact on the subsequent Enlightenment thought forms - starting from Rousseau, who essentially combined both ideas and shaped what became the foundation of modern democracy.

64. From Eyeglasses to Microscopes

An accomplished optician, Zacharias Janssen was often experimenting with different lenses, which is what fueled his curiosity to investigate the different uses of magnifying lenses. These lenses were created for reading back in the century and were much improved by the 16th century; it took Janssen's curiosity for them to gain a new function. Working alongside his father Hans, Zacharias discovered that if held under the right angle, reading spectacles can help a person show what they couldn't see with the naked eye. Wondering how to enhance the effect, Zacharias set on to construct a device using magnifying lenses. As described by Janssen's friend, Dutch diplomat William Boreel, this device was set on a brass tripod, measured about 2 and ½ feet in length, and resembled a dolphin. It had a 1-2 inch wide brass tube attached to a lens on one and an ebony disc on its other end. At first, no one paid much attention to Janssen's bizarre invention because they had no idea what he did. His friends and acquaintances considered it a quirky hobby until Cornelis Drebbel, another Dutch inventor, saw it and started spreading the word to his influential friends. This is how the French court physician learned about it, too, and started questioning where the invention came from.

It was also revealed that Janssen built several of these devices and they would be later named microscopes. Some had three tubes instead of one, with two being smaller and could be slid into the third one. Each tube had different lenses on its ends, providing diverse magnifying capabilities. The most advanced models had a bi-convex eyepiece and could magnify objects 3-9 times. Interestingly, these had no mounting mechanism, which meant Janssen could carry them wherever he went and try them out on the go.

65. Bizarre Air Pump Experiments

When Otto von Guericke created his first air pump prototype in 1650, he had no idea it would serve as the source of unusual entertainment a decade or so later. It all began when Robert Boyle, the son of a wealthy nobleman in Cork, commissioned a similar device to see how it worked. Being a scientifically oriented person, Boyle was always conducting experiments, which led to him getting the air pump in 1659. While denoting the first one to the Royal Society, he commissioned two more, this time with specific instructions. However, this meant that he could operate them with the help of their manufacturer, Robert Hooke. Despite this, the duo often did public demonstrations of this strange invention, devising the most highly criticized and often questionable experiments.

Moreover, as described in Boyle's later publication, "*New Experiments Physico-Mechanical, Touching the Spring of the Air, and its Effects,*" it also helped him learn a lot about the properties of air. They tested regular and rarified air and its effects on barometers, combustion, sound, and even magnetism. While these led to great scientific discoveries, Boyle didn't stop there. He also began testing how rarified air and the lack of air affect living beings. By locking animals in a confined space and sucking the air out of this space, he demonstrated that living beings require air for survival. The problem was that after his public demonstration of this experiment, others followed suit and started treating the experiment as a source of entertainment they could sell. This bizarre method was immortalized in a 1768 oil-on-canvas painting called "An Experiment on a Bird in the Air Pump," created by Joseph Wright of Derby. Besides the public demonstrations done by scientists, more and more people started to buy their air pumps and do their experiments at home out of amusement.

Questions to Reflect on

1. Fake news about scientific discoveries is still common in modern times. What do you think of this phenomenon?

2. Could the restorative effects of Mesmerism have some truth to them as some sort of alternative healing method?

3. What do you think of the struggle Galileo, Newton, and other scientists of the Enlightenment suffered as they tried to prove theories that went against religious beliefs?

4. What's your opinion about the significance of the social contract and natural rights as the basis of modern democratic society?

Chapter 7: Victorian England: Steam, Schemes and Surreal Kings and Queens (1801-1900 CE)

The Victorian era mostly took place under the reign of Queen Victoria and lasted until her death. This period changed the course of history in Great Britain with new and exciting innovations and discoveries. It was a great time for the nation that saw Britain expanding and becoming one of the most powerful empires in the world.

The Victorian era mostly took place under the reign of Queen Victoria.
https://commons.wikimedia.org/wiki/File:Queen_Victoria_-_Winterhalter_1859.jpg

Many inventions took place at the time and defined the era, like bicycles, typewriters, motorcars, and telephones. Railways expanded, more people were moving to the city like never before, and art and literature were flourishing. The greatest authors and poets in the world came from this era, like Charles Dickens, Emily Brontë, Oscar Wilde, and Elizabeth Browning.

The Victorian era was filled with great moments, and behind each one are amazing and even stranger stories.

66. The Great Stink

Can you imagine living in a stinky town? Wherever you go, there is no escape from smelling bad odor. This is exactly what Londoners went through during the 19th century.

London's River Thames is one of the largest and most significant rivers in the city. However, it was used as a dumping ground for human and animal waste. The Victorians couldn't predict how dangerous their actions towards the river were until it was too late.

In the summer of 1858, the smell of human excrement spread throughout London, making life hard for everyone. This was one of the few incidents when the rich and poor were suffering together. It was called "The Great Stink." Imagine the women walking in London with their hankies to their noses in disgust and the men running around the city trying to get home as fast as they could to escape the stench.

It wasn't just the odor that bothered people, but the river became a health hazard. There were incidents of vomiting and fainting when people walked by it. Charles Dickens even described it as "a deadly sewer."

During this time, London was suffering from one of the hottest summers ever recorded at the time. Even Queen Victoria described the heat as "stifling." This made the stench much worse.

The odor reached the Houses of Parliament and made it impossible for people to go about their work. The only solution was to soak the curtains in lime chloride to make the smell tolerable.

The situation kept getting worse, so the Lords and the members of parliament got together and tried to find a solution. In July 1858, orders were given, and about 200 tons of lime were thrown into the river on a regular basis for a whole year in an attempt to disinfect the water.

The English people didn't want to face a similar problem in the future. So, the government hired engineer Joseph Bazalgette to create a new drainage system. The Victorians stopped polluting the Thames, and in a few years, it became one of the cleanest rivers in the world, providing the whole city with fresh water. People still use his waste management to this day.

67. Queen Victoria's Royal Rat Catcher

Stinky rivers weren't the only issue in the Victorian era. They also suffered from a rat infestation. These small creatures were causing serious problems all over the country by clogging up drains, eating people's food and crops, scaring women and children, and passing around diseases. Farmers started working together to save and protect their lands. There were also "rat vigilantes" whom people hired to help get rid of their rat problem.

However, one man stood out from the rest and was immortalized in history. He became the rats' number one enemy; he was the people's Superman, and the rats were his Lex Luther. This man was Jack Black, Rat-Catcher to Her Majesty, The Queen.

Jack was a rat expert. He didn't only catch them, but he made a business by breeding some of these unusual-colored animals and selling them as pets. Many Victorians loved pretty rats and were willing to pay a large sum of money for what he called "fancy rats." There weren't many other breeders in the country, which made Jack's services highly in demand. Even Queen Victoria sought his help.

He was so good at his job that everyone knew who he was. He became a celebrity, and people were recommending him to one another saying that "no one else can eliminate your rat problem than Jack Black." His reputation resembled that of a superhero or a magician.

Jack wasn't a regular rat catcher. Everything about him was fascinating. He had the ability to put his hands in a cage full of rats without getting bitten. He wore a custom scarlet waistcoat decorated with a rat belt buckle, a green coat, and white leather pants. His interesting outfit caught the attention of journalist Henry Mayhew, who ran a column on him in his encyclopedic series.

The journalist described him as a man in his mid-40s with gray hair and dark, thick eyebrows. He was courageous and confident. His body was covered in scars from the many rats he had caught. He told the journalist that he was bitten on every part of his body and that a rat once broke his finger.

Jack took his job very seriously, and it paid off hundreds of years later, and people are still talking about his achievements.

68. The Mummy Mania

Back in the day, the elite had some peculiar tastes and hobbies. In the Victorian era, people were fascinated, some even say obsessed, with Ancient Egypt. They were so fascinated with mummies that they hosted "unwrapping parties." They would gather and watch the unwrapping of Ancient Egyptian mummies to entertain their guests.

This fascination started in 1789 when Napoleon Bonaparte journeyed to Egypt and ignited the European's interest in Egyptology. In the 19th century, English people started traveling to Egypt to bring real ancient mummies for their unwrapping parties.

The purpose of these parties changed over the years. They used to be public medical events for doctors to study corpses. In 1834, Dr. Thomas Pettigrew unwrapped an Ancient Egyptian corpse at the Royal College of Surgeons. However, many believe that the medical element was only a facade and that this event was mainly for entertainment.

Later, they forwent the medical façade and they stopped pretending they unwrapped the mummies for science. These parties were for entertainment and thrills. Rich people showed off their status by buying an expensive mummy and throwing a big banquet with only the best food and drinks.

Whether they took place in public or private, no one ever turned down an invite to these luxurious parties. The thrill and excitement of watching an ancient corpse unwrapped was like no other.

So why were the English people really fascinated with unwrapping mummies? Well, many of them were hoping the mummy would come to life. They were basically looking for some action.

69. A Divorce Alternative

In the Victorian era, marriage was indeed until "death do us part." Only the very rich could get a divorce through the parliament, which wasn't very easy. However, love doesn't always last forever. The flame fizzles and passion dies. So what could a man do when he fell out of love with his wife? Well, he had to find an alternative to get rid of her.

A navy (or laborer) from Stacksteads, Lancashire, missed the single life and wanted to leave his wife. He decided to get creative and find a way to separate from her without a divorce. So what did he do? He offered his wife up for sale. He held an auction to sell her to the highest bidder. He didn't stop there. He actually had the auction at their matrimonial home.

Many people were curious and gathered to watch. The husband stood before them, lecturing about how women were more precious than diamonds and gold, hoping his words would impact them and someone would pay a high price for his wife.

Only one man was willing to pay an acceptable price for the poor woman. However, the husband was greedy, so he offered his kids for sale as well to sweeten the deal, but the man refused.

Don't feel bad for the wife, though. She was happy to leave her horrible husband and start a new life. Luckily, her buyer wasn't a total stranger. He was their neighbor.

These auctions weren't new to Victorian society. They became the only way men could separate from their wives. However, they were very humiliating. Husbands put lead ropes on their wives and stood in a public space, basically telling everyone they didn't want their wives anymore and were looking for "buyers." One could only imagine how the women felt at the time.

70. Queen Victoria's Assassination Attempts

Queen Victoria was the second longest-reigning British monarch after Queen Elizabeth II. However, she would have had a much shorter reign if some people had their way. Several attempts were made on her life. Luckily, she survived them all. In 1840, an 18-year-old boy called Edward Oxford made the first attempt on the queen by firing at her carriage. The man was quickly arrested and charged with committing high treason.

In 1842, two men shot at the queen but failed and were arrested. In 1849, an Irish immigrant attacked her carriage, but he was banished for seven years. The last attempt made on the queen's life was in March 1882. Roderick Maclean was a poet and a troubled man. He tried to assassinate the queen eight times, but he was finally arrested and spent the rest of his life in an asylum.

All these incidents did nothing but endear Queen Victoria more to her people and garnered many supporters.

71. Death Pictures

Victorian post-mortem family picture.

Some stories are strange, but this one is downright creepy. The Victorians had a weird fascination with death. This is understandable since many fatal diseases like cholera, typhus, rubella, diphtheria, scarlet fever, and measles were common at the time. So, how did the families deal with the loss of a loved one? Did they save a keepsake to remember them by? Well, some did that, while others resorted to something more bizarre.

In the Victorian era, photography was still new and not very common. Only a few could afford it. For this reason, they only used this technology on special occasions or when tragic events happened. When they lost a loved one, they immortalized their memory by taking photographs.

You probably think they took photographs of their loved ones before they died to look back at their sweet memories together. Well, what happened was far more disturbing.

After a person died, they weren't buried right away. They were kept at home to allow their families to mourn and say their goodbyes. During this time, they staged photographs with the dead. They would dress them up as if they were alive, and everyone else in the family would pose with them. Parents put their dead children on their laps, and children posed next to their dead parents. They even painted eyes on the photos to make them look alive.

These pictures weren't only creepy but tragic, too. Imagine the only picture you have of your loved one is when they are dead.

72. Grave Robbing Career

Nowadays, marketeers and influencers are some of the hottest careers, but during the Victorian era, grave robbing was pretty common. As you know, medical students must learn on cadavers, and Victorian students were no different. However, they faced some difficulties. The government only allowed them to use the corpses of criminals who were executed.

In 1823, only a few crimes were punished by execution, so medical students couldn't find enough cadavers for practice. They decided to hire grave robbers, or resurrectionists, as they were called at the time, to steal bodies for them. They were paid for each body they got while others were kept on retainer. Dentists also hired resurrectionists to steal teeth from corpses.

Fresh dead corpses were highly in demand, but with the rise of grave robbery, security increased in cemeteries. So, resurrectionists had to get creative. Rather than stealing fresh bodies, they killed people and delivered them as cadavers.

73. The Agapemonites

When you think of Victorians, you typically imagine reserved people who don't usually express their emotions. Can you imagine their shock and disapproval when a free-love cult arrived in London?

A reverend called Henry Prince claimed he was possessed and threw a dramatic performance every Sunday to show the people that something had a hold on him. The Victorians were curious, and many flocked to the church every week to see him.

One day, he told the people that he absorbed the spirit of the Lord. The church responded by stripping him of his titles, but this didn't put an end to his shenanigans. He started a cult of mainly rich unmarried women. He convinced them to give up all their worldly possessions to him so he could buy "The Abode of Love." This was a group of cottages surrounded by a 12-foot wall.

His main donors were the Nottidge sisters, five unmarried sisters whom he married off to five of his followers. However, these weren't ordinary marriages but spiritual ones. Married men and women were commanded to remain celibate. However, some of his followers didn't abide by his rules.

In fact, Prince didn't practice what he preached. He used to perform multiple sex rituals in public. One of them was with a virgin and took place on a billiard table. This lewd act ended up losing him a few followers, but the cult was still going strong.

Clearly, Prince was insane. He even claimed that he was immortal, but his death in 1889 proved him wrong. John Hugh Smyth-Pigott took his place, and he also claimed that he was the Second Coming and immortal, but he died in 1927. In 1956, the cult disappeared forever.

74. Corpse Medicine

Corpse medicine is a type of remedy for all types of diseases, and it's more disturbing than you think. Victorians believed that if they consumed parts of a corpse, they would miraculously heal. One of the most popular treatments for apoplexy was mixing chocolate with a human skull. Surprise, surprise, it didn't work.

Although this type of medicine was common in the 16th and 17th centuries, it reached its highest popularity in the Victorian era. Many books were published on the subject with recipes to prepare remedies from corpses.

Executioners benefited so much from this "business." They prided themselves as both bringers of death and healers. They sold the blood of the people they executed to the poor who were suffering from various ailments.

You should be grateful that your doctor sends you to a pharmacy and not an executioner.

75. Ghosts or Hallucinations?

The Victorian era was a time of innovation and advancements in various areas. One of the biggest and most significant inventions at the time was indoor light fixtures. The people were slowly moving away from candlelight and embracing the first signs of innovation. However, it didn't come for free.

These lights worked with gas, and because many people were using them, it put undue pressure on the gas lines, leading to fires and explosions. Dangerous gasses also leaked at homes like carbon monoxide, sulfur, hydrogen, and methane. Since most windows at the time were covered with heavy drapes and there wasn't proper ventilation, the gas affected people's health. This could explain why Victorians used to faint a lot.

The gas also released toxic fumes, causing hallucinations. Many people under the effect of the gas believed they saw ghosts. This led to the spread of ghost stories that many Victorians believed were real.

76. King George IV's Rollercoaster Romance

King George IV was Queen Victoria's uncle. When he was born, he became the Prince of Wales. He was a charming and well-mannered young man – *but he had a very scandalous love life.*

King George IV was Queen Victoria's uncle.
https://commons.wikimedia.org/wiki/File:George_IV_bust1.jpg

When he was a young man, he met Maria Fitzherbert, who was twice widowed. It was love at first sight for the prince, who asked her to become his mistress right away. Maria was shocked by the request, for she was a Catholic and a religious woman and refused to live in sin. So the prince asked her to marry him. George cut himself in front of his beloved in a fit of passion to show her that he couldn't live without her. Maria had no choice but to accept the crazy-in-love prince's proposal.

In 1785, the couple got married but kept it a secret because the prince broke a few rules to marry his beloved. Royal members under the age of 25 must ask for the king's permission before they got married which he didn't do, making their marriage illegal. Maria was also a Catholic, and the law forbade Catholics from sitting on the throne. This was going to wreak havoc when he became king. The queen should sit on the throne by her husband's side, but the law made it impossible. Maria was also a widow, and she would never be accepted by the royal family as they preferred virgin brides. However, nothing could keep the prince from the woman he loved, and they continued their affair for many years. George wasn't discreet, and many people knew of their secret marriage.

The prince had a very expensive taste, and he spent his money on his stables, entertaining his guests, and decorating his homes. This left him with a huge debt. He had no choice but to ask the parliament for help. They agreed, but on one condition: he had to leave his wife and marry his Protestant cousin Caroline of Brunswick. He agreed and left Maria.

It was clear from the moment George saw Caroline that their marriage would fail. On their first meeting, George got drunk and Caroline found his behavior unacceptable. She also wasn't physically attracted to him and didn't find him handsome. On their wedding day, the prince couldn't stop drinking.

Their marriage didn't last, and the couple separated. The young prince quickly returned to the arms of his beloved Maria.

The Victorians had very peculiar habits. From unwrapping parties to their death pictures and corpse medicine, you can't help but wonder what else you don't know about this fascinating society. Interestingly, in an era that brought to the world some of the most powerful literary works and creative inventions, the people still had uncivilized beliefs and traditions. However, this is what makes any society intriguing: there is always more than what meets the eye.

Questions to Reflect on:

1. What do you think of unwrapping parties, and what do they say about the elite Victorian's morals?

2. If divorce wasn't an option, what would you do to end your marriage with your partner?

3. What do you think of the "Death Pictures" story? Is it creepy or tragic?

4. Why do you think unmarried women were easy prey for a man like Prince?

5. Would you eat a part of a corpse if it would save your life?

6. Would you marry someone you don't love to please your family or to get out of a bad situation?

Chapter 8: The 20th Century (1901-2000CE)

The 21st century is one of the most impactful periods as it relates to how the modern world has been shaped. The invention of the World Wide Web, cloning, commercialized electricity, public feud, test tube babies, celebrity obsession, and so much more have all contributed to making the 21st century a crazy time to live in! The technological and industrial acceleration experience at the time created new platforms for expression and freedom that never existed before. This century also saw many marginalized groups demanding their representation in society, which came with revolutionary cultural shifts. Therefore, the 21st century can be seen as a transition from older systems by way of radical to what is considered normal today.

The bravery to experiment, question, and challenge the status quo are the defining characteristics of this key century in human development. As the modern world dives further into technological progress at a faster pace than ever before and people engage with new cultural frameworks, it becomes clear that contemporary society is primarily formed from the spillover of the 21st century. The weird world-defining occurrences from the 1900s up until 2000 must be considered when examining human progress. Dive deep into the crazy, inspiring, and shocking mess of the 21st century to see how progress, freedom, and equality can arise from chaotic environments.

77. Tesla and Edison

Nikola Tesla preferred working with AC electrical currents.
https://commons.wikimedia.org/wiki/File:Tesla_Sarony.jpg

Public feuds are very common today as big names post recklessly on social media, but the grandfather of public relations battles in a relatively modern form is Nikola Tesla versus Thomas Edison. Unlike many pseudo-intellectuals and political pundits who spar it out on social media, Tesla and Edison were both legitimate geniuses. The main friction between the two was the differing opinions on science. One of their disagreements that is often highlighted is Tesla's preference for working with AC electrical currents, while Edison promoted the use of DC, which he invented. Although Tesla, at one point, ended up working for Edison, this disagreement made them constantly bash one another's credibility publicly.

The single craziest moment in their rivalry happened in 1903 when Edison electrocuted an elephant to show how dangerous AC currents were. The act of killing animals with electricity was a common stunt in Edison's traveling demonstrations, but the elephant at the Luna Park

Zoo was by far the most attention-grabbing. Tesla died penniless due to a string of bad business decisions, while Edison went on to amass a vast fortune. Although Edison's public relations stunts were impressive, his DC soon fell out of favor as more households began installing AC currents. Today, both Nikola Tesla and Thomas Edison are highly respected in the scientific field for their revolutionary contributions to technology.

78. The Disappearance of Amelia Earhart

The tragic disappearance of Amelia Earhart morphed into a fertile forest of speculation and conspiracy theories that spanned decades. Earhart attempted the incredible feat of being the first female to fly across the Atlantic Ocean by herself. Earhart went missing in 1937, and about a year and a half later, she was declared dead after an intense search conducted by the military. Earhart was a skilled and famous pilot who made a lucrative career completing many publicity stunts. Her body was never discovered, so many people began speculating what happened to her, especially after the government had halted their search.

The most logical explanation is that her plane ran out of fuel, so she crashed, but that was too simple for people to accept as true because she was such an amazing pilot. One of the most popular conspiracy theories that emerged was that Earhart was captured by the Japanese, who were the WWII enemies of the United States. Archeologists in the 90s found bones in the Phoenix Islands that they theorized might be the remains of Earhart, but this theory is disputed because there were no plane parts found near the discovery. The latest in the Amelia Earhart saga was billionaire Ted Waitt funding an expedition to the sea floor of the coast of Howland Island in an attempt to find some parts of the plane or even remnants of Earhart. To this day, no one has found the plane or her body, so the fatal disappearance is still shrouded in darkness.

79. Beatlemania and Beyond

It's hard to capture how insanely popular The Beatles were, but the fact that their obsessive fans created a wild phenomenon known as Beatlemania should provide a clue. The Liverpool natives came from humble backgrounds to grow into one of the most influential bands of all time. The obsession with The Beatles was at its peak between the years of 1963 and 1966. The band's hype grew steadily in England and spread across the world with their live performance on "The Ed Sullivan Show" in 1964. Beatlemania can be seen as one of the first weird moments which the obsessive culture of modern celebrity fanatics originated from. Wherever The Beatles toured, they were met with droves of mostly female teenage fans who would do anything just for a glimpse of their favorite idols.

At the height of the Beatlemania phenomenon, they could hardly play shows. Their fans would continuously scream so loud throughout their set that you would not be able to hear any of the music. Imagine going to listen to a band and instead hear frantic screaming for an hour without any pause. Supporters of the group would rush to buy anything related to The Beatles, from lunchboxes to posters and clothing, as girls declared who their favorites in the band were. Fan culture became a staple in the entertainment world from there onwards, with boy bands being worshiped, from The Backstreet Boys in the 90s up to the K-Pop stars of today. The internet fuels fan obsessions because people feel like they have more access to their favorite celebrities, but it all began in the 1960s with the bowl-cut-wearing, genre-defining, lovable band from the UK.

80. Christiaan Barnard's Two-Headed Dog

Christiaan Barnard was a South African surgeon who successfully completed the first heart transplant in 1967. The patient lived for 18 days, eventually passing away from bilateral pneumonia. Barnard's contributions to the medical field greatly impacted the development of organ transplants and heart surgeries. However, as is often the case, great men have some eccentricities. Barnard attributed much of the development of transplantation to Vladimir Demikhov, a Russian surgeon who had created a two-headed dog and achieved some huge leaps in heart surgery, namely being the first person to perform coronary artery bypass on a mammal. Barnard's arrogance, or confidence, drove him to immediately recreate the experiment, which he paraded around the medical school he was a part of. Nobody knows exactly why the famed surgeon would do this other than to prove he could.

Maybe it was some form of hero worship, but the ethically reprehensible act of creating a two-headed dog had no medical use for Barnard. Although it takes a lot of technical skill to create such an abomination, it is unclear why anybody would want to do it. Considering that Barnard was a respected and serious surgeon, engaging in these kinds of experiments seems somewhat out of character. Once he had completed his first heart transplant, Barnard gained international acclaim and traveled the world to show surgeons how to replicate his success. There were many deaths along the way due to lesser skilled surgeons attempting what Barnard did, as well as inadequate training and preparation. The road to medical marvels always seems to be paved with tragic losses, but their sacrifices propelled the world into a more advanced age in medicine.

81. Dolly the Sheep

Since you already have two-headed dogs on your mind, maybe a nice palette cleanser would be a discussion of cloned sheep. Biologist Ian Wilmut cloned a Finn Dorset sheep using its mammary glands. In 1996, Dolly was born as a scientific marvel. When the sheep was revealed to the public, it caused a media frenzy. Some feared that science was going too far, and others celebrated the possibilities that came along with this advancement. Dolly's body is now in the National Museum of Scotland in Edinburgh. Although Dolly was not the first sheep that Wilmut's team had cloned at The Roslin Institute, what made the sheep special was that she was cloned using cells from an adult, which researchers believed was not possible at the time.

Dolly the Sheep was a clone.
Toni Barros from São Paulo, Brasil, CC BY-SA 2.0 <https://creativecommons.org/licenses/by-sa/2.0>, via Wikimedia Commons:
https://commons.wikimedia.org/wiki/File:Dolly_face_closeup.jpg

Dolly's cloning was important because it opened up knowledge about how stem cells could be used in various medical implementations. After all, adult cells were able to produce a fully-fledged, functioning sheep. The cloning process was not flawless because Dolly aged faster than other sheep. Scientists who worked on the project theorized that this may have been a result of the adult cells that were used in the cloning process. The existence of Dolly brings up many ethical questions in medicine about how far scientists should be allowed to explore before it breaches boundaries that should not be crossed. Dolly birthed a few lambs before eventually dying from a virus that caused lung cancer in sheep that many of the animals at the institute had contracted. The applications of cloning and stem cell research that are linked to the process continue today as people aim to find novel ways to combat the ailments and illnesses that plague humans and other organisms.

82. Test Tube Baby

From animal experimentation in the form of two-headed dogs and cloned sheep, it's time to leapfrog to the biology of humans. In 1978, Louise Brown was born as the world's first "test-tube baby." Louise Brown was born using a process called in-vitro fertilization, or IVF, which is when eggs extracted from a woman's ovaries are fertilized outside of the womb to create embryos. Today, IVF is used by many couples who experience trouble conceiving or for people who have medical conditions that would make pregnancy dangerous. The phrase "test-tube baby" creates some misconceptions about the process of IVF because it creates images of a baby being grown to viability in a lab. However, the process works very differently. The fertilized embryos through IVF are then implanted in the mother's womb, who will eventually give birth to the baby a mere nine months later.

The public came to know about Louise Brown and her family by way of a documentary called "To Mrs Brown... A Daughter" that aired on ITV. What really captured the public about the story was how normal the parents, Lesley and John Brown, seemed because they were conservative-looking and managed a typical household for 1970s norms. Not everyone was on board with Louise's atypical birth. Religious leaders raised objections as fears grew about the unknown results, and theological implications considered a baby born in this way was "unnatural." Louise is still alive and was able to conceive children of her own. Louise published a popular biography that capture the details of her interesting existence called *Louise Brown: My Life As The World's First Test-Tube Baby.*

83. The World Wide Web

The defining invention of the 21st century is arguably the World Wide Web. Considering how the web is used today, it is shocking to realize that it was intended for scientists, universities, and researchers to be able to share information over long distances. Today, it is used for pointless online fights, conspiracy theories, celebrity gossip, and for influencers to have a way to scam their fans into buying worthless crypto coins. Tim Berners-Lee invented the technology while working for CERN in 1989. Berners-Lee was born in London to parents who were computer scientists so it seems that he was destined for the path he took since birth. From a young age, Berners-Lee was interested in gadgets and constantly played with model trains as he found their mechanics intriguing.

Instead of going for a corporate route and looking to sell the 'internet' and gatekeep it so that he could make billions, Berners-Lee was a true revolutionary who realized that he needed to allow everyone to have access to the technology for it to fully flourish into the life-changing invention that it later became. The CERN institute made the code available royalty-free, which allowed several geniuses to jump on the idea and express their creativity with this new medium. The fundamental principles that were developed when the web first started are still in place today, as the internet is a decentralized technology that anyone can use without specific permission from an overarching corporate read. The internet radically changed how people share, produce, and consume information away from big-budget media conglomerates and governmental institutions into the hands of everyday people.

84. Tulsa Race Massacre

In the decades that followed the abolition of slavery, African Americans began rising socio-economically and establishing themselves as autonomous, ambitious people. They built many prosperous cities, and some became successful businesspeople. The neighborhood of Greenwood in Tulsa, Oklahoma, was so prosperous that it became known as Black Wall Street. The roads were lined with all kinds of businesses, including grocery stores, doctor's offices, and nightclubs. The end of slavery did not signal the end of bigotry, so many white people in the surrounding areas grew jealous of the new prosperity that black communities, like Tulsa, were experiencing. This fueled their hatred so much that they decided to organize a heavily armed group of people to drive the black population out of Tulsa and destroy all the businesses that they had worked so hard to establish.

Many people died in the horrific massacre, showing that the work to demand equality for black people was far from finished. To make the loss even more devastating, local and national media covered up the atrocity, and it was not recorded by national or state history organizations. Many of the residents fled, but the few that stayed behind kept the memory of Greenwood alive in whispers. Today, Greenwood is held up as a beacon of potential for black economic growth and liberation, as well as a symbol of the systemic oppression African Americans continue to face. The number of people who died in the riot is unknown, with estimates spanning from 70 to 300. It is nearly impossible to determine the true extent of the murderous plundering because many people were buried in unmarked graves.

85. Vietnam War Protests

Anti-Vietnam protests.
The Tribune / SEARCH Foundation, CC BY 4.0
<*https://creativecommons.org/licenses/by/4.0*>, *via Wikimedia Commons:*
https://commons.wikimedia.org/wiki/File:Anti-
Vietnam_War_protest_March_from_U.S._Consulate_7_Wynyard_Street_to_Hyde_Park,_Sydn
ey,_NSW_09.jpg

During WWII, the public support for the troops was unmatched, with civilians making many personal sacrifices to support the war effort and many works of art being positive military propaganda. However, the same cannot be said of the widely unpopular Vietnam War. People had just come out of a world war a few decades earlier and were not keen on repeating the devastation that left all sides broken and wounded. The war in Vietnam was meant to stop the spread of a communist government that had recently defeated French colonial forces. Too many US citizens who had seen their soldiers returning from service damaged and broken and who had also seen images of the catastrophic destruction that resulted as a consequence of US occupation considered the war unacceptable.

The height of the war saw soldiers becoming drug-addicted, traumatized, and apathetic. The flower power hippie movement was primarily driven by the antiwar stance, as well as the use of illicit hallucinogenic substances. Vietnam War veterans spoke about how much they were hated when they returned, stating that people yelled curse words and even spat at them. Some soldiers joined the protest movement upon their return, having experienced mental and physical injuries from the war. Artists and musicians got on board to produce classic protest songs like Marvin Gaye's "What's Going On." or John Lennon's "Imagine." Due to the constant antiwar narrative, as well as the diminishing benefits of the continued fight in 1973, the war officially ended.

86. The Red Scare

Following the end of WWII, the Soviet Union and the United States engaged in a global Cold War as two emerging superpowers that did not trust one another. Proxy wars were fought all around the world as the economic and political systems of communism and capitalism battled it out. In the 1940s, as well as the early 1950s, fear that communists would take over the United States, as well as nuclear threats, became a prominent concern among the US population and its government.

U.S. Senator Joseph R. McCarthy began a crusade against those who he believed were infiltrators looking to promote communism on US shores. McCarthy leveled claims of being a communist traitor against celebrities, public officials, and intellectuals. He also created a silencing and fear tactic as well as political repression known as "McCarthyism." Lawyer Joseph Welch, alongside some of McCarthy's colleagues, put an end to the intimidation tactics of the senator in the Army-McCarthy hearings. During the Red Scare, communism was demonized and is still frowned upon in US politics to this day. Many people installed nuclear bunkers in their homes and ran nuclear safety drills in schools, fearing that the Soviet Union would attack. Red Scare tactics are reemerging as China becomes a growing political and economic threat to the US.

87. The Satanic Panic

Whereas the Red Scare was highly politically influenced, the Satanic Panic was more of a social movement. In the 1980s and 1990s, growing fear that people were targeting children with Satanist and occult propaganda permeated the culture. False claims of satanic ritual abuse that were coerced out of people using hypnosis started a pushback against all materials that were deemed demonic.

Conspiracy theories began spreading that Rock music icons were hiding messages in their songs if you played their records backward. Board games like Dungeons and Dragons also came under fire for their mystical imagery and magical themes. People took to the streets to burn books, games, and records in protest to the devil they believed was after their children. These kinds of mass hysteria are still prevalent today, with people believing that musicians and actors are part of Satanic baby-eating cults.

88. Stonewall Riots

The 21st century was a time of massive social reforms around race and culture. The LGBT community was also a part of these reforms as they began demanding their rights. The gay rights movement kicked off with what is today known as the Stonewall Riots. After police raided a club called The Stonewall Inn in Greenwich Village, New York, a riot began in response to the brutality that the LGBT community was experiencing. The riot began a chain reaction that fueled protest in the week that followed. Same-sex relations were illegal at the time in New York. The activism that followed the Stonewall Riot changed the lives of modern LGBT people, who do not have to experience the same kinds of legal oppression that they once did.

Questions to Reflect on

1. Why do you think people fall into conspiracy frenzies like the Red Scare or the Satanic Panic?

2. How far do you think scientists should be allowed to go when it comes to experimenting with life? Are there ethical lines that should be drawn?

3. How does public organizing and outcry affect government policy-making?

4. Do you think the culture of celebrity worship is good or bad for society? Why do you think so?

Chapter 9: Digital Dilemmas: Strange Moments from the Tech Age to the Modern Day (2000-Present)

The 21st century has ushered in remarkable technological advancements and global connectivity. From the proliferation of smartphones to the rise of social media platforms and the emergence of artificial intelligence, this world has undergone a digital transformation unlike anything witnessed in previous centuries. These innovations have undoubtedly brought about convenience, efficiency, and the promise of a brighter future. However, amidst these incredible breakthroughs, there have also emerged peculiar challenges and oddities that define the modern age.

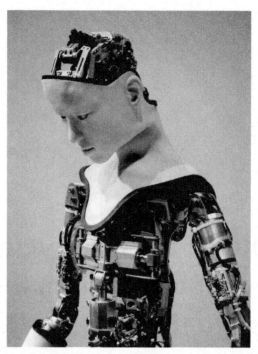

The 21ˢᵗ century witnessed the emergence of artificial intelligence.

This chapter invites you to navigate this ever-evolving digital labyrinth. It shines a spotlight on the peculiarities that have emerged amidst groundbreaking technological advancements. As you journey through these strange and captivating moments, you'll witness the extraordinary creativity of the digital age and confront the dilemmas and oddities that have surfaced alongside its unparalleled progress. So, fasten your seatbelt and prepare to explore the unexpected in this riveting odyssey through the digital wonders.

Setting the Stage for the 21st Century

The 21ˢᵗ century has been a time of unprecedented technological progress. Here's an overview of some key developments that have shaped this era:

- **Rapid Advancements in Communication:** The advent of the internet, coupled with the creation of smartphones, has connected people globally like never before. Communication has become instantaneous, allowing people to bridge geographical gaps and share information at the speed of light.

- **Social Media Revolution:** Social media platforms like Facebook, Twitter, Instagram, and TikTok have revolutionized the way you interact and share your life. These platforms have created a virtual social landscape where trends, news, and opinions spread rapidly, influencing public discourse and shaping culture.
- **Artificial Intelligence (AI):** The rise of AI has transformed industries ranging from healthcare to finance. AI-powered technologies now drive everything from voice assistants like Siri and Alexa to self-driving cars and predictive analytics. These advancements have promised increased efficiency and convenience but have also raised questions about privacy and ethics.
- **E-commerce Boom:** Online shopping and e-commerce giants, like Amazon, have revolutionized the way you shop. The convenience of ordering products with a click has transformed retail, but it has also raised concerns about the impact on local businesses and the exploitation of workers in the gig economy.

89. The Peculiarities Amidst Breakthroughs

While the 21st century has undoubtedly delivered groundbreaking technological innovations, it has also introduced peculiar challenges and oddities:

- **Digital Addiction:** With the constant connectivity offered by smartphones and social media, many individuals find themselves grappling with digital addiction. The compulsion to check notifications, scroll through endless feeds, and binge-watch online content has raised concerns about the impact on mental health and real-world relationships.
- **Misinformation and Fake News:** The ease with which information spreads online has given rise to misinformation and fake news. Sorting fact from fiction has become a daily challenge, affecting public discourse and even influencing elections and public policy.
- **Privacy Concerns:** As technology has advanced, so have concerns about digital privacy. The collection and monetization of personal data by tech companies have sparked debates about individual privacy rights and the need for robust data protection

regulations.

- **Social Isolation:** Paradoxically, while people are more connected than ever online, some individuals experience heightened social isolation in their physical lives. The allure of virtual relationships and digital interactions leads to reduced face-to-face social engagement.
- **Tech-Induced Stress:** The constant bombardment of information and the pressure to keep up with the latest trends and developments in the tech world have contributed to tech-induced stress. This stress can manifest as anxiety, FOMO (fear of missing out), and burnout.

90. Elon Musk and His Tweets: A Phenomenon Unveiled

Elon Musk is the visionary behind Tesla.

Elon Musk, the enigmatic entrepreneur and visionary behind companies like Tesla, SpaceX, and Neuralink, is a name that resonates in the tech world like no other. His influence extends far beyond the boardrooms and laboratories, and one of his most potent tools for shaping the narrative is Twitter (now called X). It's time to dive into the Elon Musk phenomenon, explore his impact on the tech industry, and examine how his tweets have become powerful catalysts for change and conversation.

The Elon Musk Phenomenon

Elon Musk's journey from co-founding Zip2 in the 1990s to becoming the CEO of multiple cutting-edge companies has been nothing short of remarkable. He is widely regarded as a pioneer in electric vehicles, space exploration, and the future of human-computer interaction. Musk's relentless pursuit of innovation and his audacious goals, such as colonizing Mars, have made him an icon of the tech age.

However, it's not just his groundbreaking ventures that have captured the public's imagination; it's his ability to engage with the world through Twitter. Musk's tweets are a unique blend of announcements, humor, and unfiltered insights into his mind. His Twitter account, with millions of followers, has become a digital window into the world of a modern tech mogul.

Tweeting the Markets

Elon Musk's tweets have transcended mere social media posts. They have become potent drivers of market dynamics and internet culture. Here are specific instances where his tweets caused ripples in the stock market and sparked online phenomena:

1. **Tesla's Stock Price Rollercoaster:** Musk's tweets about Tesla, his electric car company, have had a remarkable impact on its stock price. In 2018, Musk tweeted about taking Tesla private at $420 per share, causing the stock to surge. This tweet also led to regulatory investigations and legal challenges. His tweets about Tesla's valuation and production goals continue to sway the stock price.

2. **Cryptocurrency Tweets:** Musk's tweets about cryptocurrencies like Bitcoin and Dogecoin have caused significant market fluctuations. His endorsement of Bitcoin led to a surge in its price, while his criticism of its environmental impact caused it to plummet. Musk's humorous tweets about Dogecoin, originally created as a meme, have propelled it to become a cryptocurrency with a substantial following.

3. **GameStop and "Stonks":** During the GameStop stock frenzy of early 2021, Musk tweeted "Gamestonk!!" along with a link to the WallStreetBets Reddit forum. This tweet added fuel to the retail

investor-driven stock surge and further popularized internet memes around stock market investing, creating a unique intersection of online culture and finance.

The Influence of a Tweet

Elon Musk's tweets extend beyond market dynamics and memes. They hold profound implications for the worlds of finance, online culture, and beyond:

1. **Market Volatility:** Musk's ability to move markets with a single tweet has raised questions about the role of social media in stock trading. Regulators are increasingly vigilant about the potential manipulation of stock prices through online platforms.

2. **Online Engagement:** Musk's Twitter presence has contributed to a broader trend of influential individuals using social media as a direct channel to engage with the public and shape narratives. This shift challenges traditional communication channels and can have far-reaching consequences.

3. **Corporate Responsibility:** Musk's tweets have underscored the complex relationship between corporate leaders, their public statements, and their fiduciary responsibilities. His comments have led to legal battles and debates about the boundaries of free expression for CEOs.

Elon Musk's tweets have transformed him from a tech titan to a cultural phenomenon. His ability to captivate audiences, move markets, and drive conversations through Twitter showcases the evolving landscape of communication in the digital age. His tweets have left an indelible mark on the tech world, reminding everyone that in the digital age, even a tweet can change the course of history.

91. The Ice Bucket Challenge Phenomenon: Making Waves for ALS

The ALS Ice Bucket Challenge is a testament to the incredible power of social media to mobilize people for a charitable cause. It originated in the summer of 2014 and quickly became a viral sensation, leaving an indelible mark on online activism and charitable campaigns.

The Origins of the Challenge

The ALS Ice Bucket Challenge had modest beginnings. It was started by Pete Frates, a former baseball player at Boston College who was given an ALS diagnosis in 2012. Frates, along with his family and friends, launched the challenge in July 2014 to raise awareness and funds for ALS research and support.

The challenge was simple yet engaging. Participants were dared to pour a bucket of ice-cold water over their heads and then nominate others to do the same or make a donation to ALS research. The campaign aimed to simulate the sensations experienced by ALS patients, whose muscles progressively weaken and often become paralyzed.

The Power of Virality

What followed was nothing short of remarkable. The Ice Bucket Challenge spread rapidly across social media platforms. Celebrities, athletes, politicians, and everyday individuals joined in, creating a groundswell of participation. The challenge's virality was fueled by its shareability and the use of popular hashtags like #IceBucketChallenge.

The campaign achieved several key milestones:

- **Raising Awareness:** Millions of people around the world became familiar with ALS, a relatively lesser-known disease. The Ice Bucket Challenge put a spotlight on ALS, educating the public about its devastating effects on individuals and families.
- **Generating Donations:** The ALS Association reported a significant surge in donations, raising over $115 million during the summer of 2014 alone. These funds were earmarked for research, patient services, and public awareness campaigns.
- **Inspiring Worldwide Imitations:** The success of the Ice Bucket Challenge inspired similar viral challenges for various causes, demonstrating the potential of social media to galvanize support for charitable endeavors.

Legacy and Lessons

The Ice Bucket Challenge left a lasting legacy in the realm of online activism and charitable campaigns. Its impact can be summarized in a few key lessons:

- **Harnessing Virality:** The challenge demonstrated that a well-designed, easily shareable campaign can harness the power of social media to drive engagement and support for a cause.
- **Raising Awareness:** The Ice Bucket Challenge showed that raising awareness is often the first step in mobilizing resources for a cause. It put ALS on the global map and increased

understanding of the disease.

- **Transparency and Accountability:** Charitable organizations need to be transparent about how donations are used. The success of the Ice Bucket Challenge highlighted the importance of assuring donors that their contributions are making a tangible difference.

The ALS Ice Bucket Challenge was a groundbreaking moment in the world of online activism. It showcased the immense potential of social media to raise awareness, generate funds, and inspire global participation in charitable causes. While the challenge itself may have subsided, its legacy endures as a testament to the incredible impact that can be achieved when the digital world unites for a common good.

92. The Mystery of Bitcoin's Creator: Satoshi Nakamoto's Enigma

In the world of cryptocurrency, few names carry as much intrigue and fascination as Satoshi Nakamoto. An enigmatic figure, Nakamoto is the mastermind behind Bitcoin, the pioneering cryptocurrency that has reshaped the landscape of digital finance. Yet, despite the immense impact of Bitcoin, the true identity of Satoshi Nakamoto remains one of the most enduring mysteries of the internet age.

The Birth of Cryptocurrency

Satoshi Nakamoto's creation, Bitcoin, emerged in 2008 with the publication of a whitepaper titled *"Bitcoin: A Peer-to-Peer Electronic Cash System."* With the help of this ground-breaking idea, a decentralized digital currency that could function without the assistance of governments or banks was established. Nakamoto created the blockchain technology behind Bitcoin, which allowed for safe and open transactions and further upended established financial institutions.

Bitcoin's significance extends beyond the realm of finance. It ignited a global movement that spawned thousands of alternative cryptocurrencies and laid the foundation for the broader blockchain revolution. Blockchain technology found applications in supply chain management, voting systems, and even the verification of art and collectibles.

The Quest for Satoshi

Despite Nakamoto's groundbreaking contributions, the creators chose to remain anonymous throughout Bitcoin's development and proliferation. Their disappearance from public view in 2011 only deepened the mystery. The quest to unveil Satoshi Nakamoto's true identity has since become a pursuit of legend.

Numerous individuals have been suspected of being Nakamoto, including computer scientists, cryptographers, and even reclusive billionaires. Yet, each lead has ultimately led to a dead end, leaving Nakamoto's identity shrouded in secrecy.

The quest for Satoshi Nakamoto has given rise to controversies, lawsuits, and ethical dilemmas. Some argue that revealing Nakamoto's identity could compromise their privacy, while others believe it is essential for transparency within the cryptocurrency space. Whether Nakamoto's true identity will ever be unveiled remains uncertain, but its legacy in the world of cryptocurrency is undeniable, leaving an indelible mark on the digital age.

93. Viral Trends and Cyber Phenomena: From "Gangnam Style" to Memes

The digital age has witnessed an explosion of viral trends and cyber phenomena that have reshaped how people consume and create content. These trends, often born on the internet, have the power to captivate global audiences, challenge societal norms, and redefine cultural expressions.

Gangnam Style and Viral Music Videos

In 2012, South Korean pop sensation Psy unleashed "Gangnam Style" upon the world, and it became an overnight sensation. With its catchy tune, quirky dance moves, and colorful visuals, the music video quickly became the most-watched video on YouTube at the time. Its impact was not just musical but cultural, as it introduced millions to K-pop and Korean culture.

Selfie Culture

The selfie has taken the world by storm.
https://www.pexels.com/photo/happy-multiethnic-friends-taking-selfie-in-street-6141099/

The rise of smartphones and social media platforms brought about the era of selfie culture. The simple act of taking a photo of oneself has become a form of self-expression, documentation, and even a means of empowerment. However, it has also raised questions about narcissism and the pursuit of perfection.

Challenges to Reality

Augmented reality games like "Pokémon Go" blurred the lines between the physical and digital worlds. Players ventured into the real world to capture virtual creatures, fostering a sense of exploration and community. This phenomenon highlighted the potential for technology to enhance physical experiences and encouraged people to engage with their surroundings in new ways. However, it also raised concerns about privacy and distracted behavior.

The Rise of Memes

Internet memes have evolved into a form of digital folklore, influencing humor, communication, and cultural references. From "Distracted Boyfriend" to "Woman Yelling at a Cat," memes have a unique ability to distill complex ideas into easily shareable and relatable images or videos. Memes have become a form of participatory culture, allowing people to collectively create and share humor in the digital realm.

Social Media and Influencer Culture: From Facebook to Kardashians

The advent of social media has fundamentally transformed the way people connect, communicate, and consume content. It has given birth to an era where ordinary individuals can become influential figures and where controversies, privacy concerns, and cancel culture loom large. Here's a deeper dive into the evolution of social media and the rise of influencer culture.

94. The Birth of Facebook

Facebook was started in 2004. S
https://commons.wikimedia.org/wiki/File:Facebook_f_logo_(2019).svg

Facebook was started in 2004 by Mark Zuckerberg and his undergraduate buddies in their Harvard dorm room. What began as a platform for university students to connect quickly evolved into a global social network. Facebook's meteoric rise brought with it questions of privacy, data security, and its impact on society. Controversies surrounding data breaches and misinformation have made it a lightning rod for scrutiny. Despite the challenges, Facebook remains a major player in the social media landscape, connecting billions worldwide.

---

95. The Kardashians and Influencer Empire

The Kardashian family, propelled to stardom by their reality TV show "Keeping Up with the Kardashians," transformed into a cultural force to be reckoned with. Kim Kardashian and her siblings leveraged their fame into an empire that included cosmetics, fashion, and endorsements. Their mastery of social media, with millions of followers each, blurred the lines between celebrity and influencer. The Kardashian phenomenon exemplifies the power of social media in elevating individuals to global recognition and the commercial success that can follow.

96. Cancel Culture

Cancel culture, a phenomenon that gained prominence in the digital age, revolves around the swift and public shaming or boycotting of individuals, often celebrities or public figures, for perceived offensive actions or statements. While cancel culture has been credited with holding people accountable for misconduct, it has also raised concerns about the erosion of free speech and the potential for online mobs to enforce conformity through fear and intimidation. The nuances of cancel culture, including its impact on personal growth and redemption, continue to be subjects of debate.

The Rise of Artificial Intelligence: Transforming Lives and Challenging Ethics

Artificial Intelligence (AI) has transitioned from science fiction to a fundamental part of everyday life. It's revolutionizing industries, improving convenience, and raising important ethical questions. It's time to explore the multifaceted impact of AI, from its integration into daily routines to the ethical dilemmas it presents and the quest for Artificial General Intelligence (AGI).

97. AI in Everyday Life

AI has merged smoothly into everyday life, frequently without your awareness. Homes have become more responsive and connected with the help of voice assistants such as Alexa and Siri, which offer real-time information and control over smart gadgets. Recommendation algorithms on platforms like Netflix and Spotify personalize your entertainment choices, enhancing your viewing and listening experiences. AI-driven chatbots assist with customer support, and facial recognition technology speeds up smartphone unlocking and even passport control at airports.

Ethical Dilemmas of AI

As AI becomes increasingly pervasive, ethical concerns have come to the forefront. One pressing issue is algorithmic bias, where AI systems discriminate due to biased data inputs. For instance, biased algorithms in writing processes can reinforce misinformation. Moreover, the potential for job displacement as AI automates certain tasks raises questions about unemployment and retraining for the workforce. Balancing the benefits of AI with these ethical concerns is an ongoing challenge.

98. The Quest for AGI

While current AI systems excel in specific tasks, achieving Artificial General Intelligence (AGI) remains a significant goal. AGI refers to AI systems that possess human-like general intelligence, the ability to understand, learn, and adapt across various domains. Researchers are actively pursuing AGI, envisioning a future where AI can think, reason, and solve problems like humans.

The journey toward AGI involves developing deep learning models, reinforcement learning, and neural networks. Companies like OpenAI and DeepMind are at the forefront of this quest, pushing the boundaries of AI research. While AGI promises remarkable advancements, it also raises ethical concerns about the potential implications of creating machines with human-like intelligence.

Viral Trends and Cyber Phenomena: TikTok, Meme Stocks, and the Metaverse

In the digital age, viral trends and cyber phenomena shape your online experiences and reflect the rapid evolution of the internet landscape. From the rise of TikTok to meme stocks and the concept of the metaverse, dive into these intriguing facets of the digital world.

99. TikTok and the Short-Form Video Revolution

TikTok has ushered in a revolution in short-form video content. This platform, known for its user-friendly interface and creative tools, has empowered individuals to become content creators and entertainers. TikTok's algorithmic magic ensures that even newcomers can go viral overnight, spawning dance challenges, lip-syncing trends, and comedic skits that resonate with global audiences. The platform's influence extends beyond the screen, impacting fashion, music, and even politics. TikTok has become a cultural force, proving that a short video can have a lasting impact.

100. Meme Stocks and Online Movements

GameStop's stock surge in early 2021 was a defining moment in the world of finance. Reddit's WallStreetBets forum, populated by amateur traders, coordinated a buying frenzy that sent the stock price soaring, challenging traditional Wall Street practices. The GameStop saga highlighted the power of internet communities to mobilize and disrupt established systems. It also spawned discussions about the potential for coordinated online movements to reshape markets.

101. The Metaverse and Virtual Reality

The concept of the metaverse has gained traction, promising a new dimension of online life. It envisions a virtual universe where individuals can interact, work, play, and create, blurring the lines between the digital and physical worlds. Companies like Meta (formerly Facebook) are investing heavily in virtual reality technologies to build the metaverse. Virtual worlds are no longer limited to gaming. They encompass social interactions, education, and commerce. As the metaverse evolves, it prompts you to reimagine the possibilities of digital existence.

The digital age is an ongoing journey. New peculiarities, challenges, and opportunities will undoubtedly emerge. The pace of technological advancement shows no signs of slowing down, and your relationship with the digital realm will continue to evolve.

Questions to Reflect on

1. How can you strike a balance between embracing the convenience of AI and addressing its ethical concerns, such as privacy and bias?

2. In what ways can online communities use their collective power for positive change beyond the realm of meme stocks and viral challenges?

3. As you venture into virtual worlds and the metaverse, what safeguards and ethical guidelines should be in place to protect user rights and privacy?

4. What responsibilities do tech companies have in addressing issues like misinformation, online harassment, and the unintended consequences of their platforms?

5. How might society adapt to the evolving nature of work in an era where automation and AI are transforming industries?

These questions invite you to contemplate the implications of digital dilemmas and engage in thoughtful discussions that will shape the way you navigate the ever-evolving tech age.

Conclusion

History is a tapestry woven with countless threads, and the moments you explored in "101 Weird Moments in Human History" are just a glimpse into the vast and peculiar landscape of the past. As you delve into these historical oddities, you'll begin to notice intriguing connections and threads that link seemingly disparate events, revealing a greater overall historical significance.

For example, consider the strange tales of Ancient Egypt and the peculiar practices of the Roman Empire. While these two civilizations existed in different times and places, they share a common thread: a fascination with the afterlife. In Egypt, the construction of elaborate tombs, mummies, and complex burial rituals reflected a belief in the eternal journey of the soul. Similarly, the Romans, with their elaborate funerary practices and belief in the importance of honoring the deceased, were deeply influenced by their unique views on the afterlife. By examining these seemingly unrelated moments, we uncover a shared human quest to understand what lies beyond our mortal existence.

As you journey through history, you'll also find that certain themes reappear, such as innovation and technology. From the steam-powered wonders of Victorian England to the strange moments of the Digital Age, there's a thread of human ingenuity that spans centuries. It's a testament to the unending human desire to improve and innovate, whether through steam engines or cutting-edge tech.

Moreover, you may notice that some of the weird moments in history reveal unexpected lessons. Take the Stone Age Stunts, for instance.

While they may seem bizarre, these early experiments with daring feats and survival techniques laid the foundation for the development of crucial skills that would shape the course of human evolution. These seemingly strange actions were, in fact, steps on the path to progress.

Whether it's the peculiar rituals of the Stone Age or the technological marvels of the 21st century, there's a common curiosity, creativity, and adaptability that runs through human history. These moments are a reminder that, regardless of the era, humans have always strived to make sense of the world around them. It's human nature to push the boundaries of what is possible and to connect through shared experiences (regardless of how bizarre they may seem).

In this sense, "101 Weird Moments in Human History" is not just a collection of stories but a reflection of our shared humanity, a testament to the enduring spirit of exploration that defines us as a species. This book serves as an invitation to embark on your historical explorations, to uncover the hidden stories and oddities that have yet to be fully explored.

Weird moments are not isolated incidents but interconnected pieces of the intricate puzzle that is our shared past. They offer glimpses into the strange, the remarkable, and the deeply human aspects of history. And while you've explored 101 of these moments, know that countless others are waiting for you to uncover. History, after all, is a never-ending journey of discovery.

If you enjoyed this book, a review on Amazon would be greatly appreciated because it would mean a lot to hear from you.

To leave a review:

1. Open your camera app.
2. Point your mobile device at the QR code.
3. The review page will appear in your web browser.

Thanks for your support!

Check out another book in the series

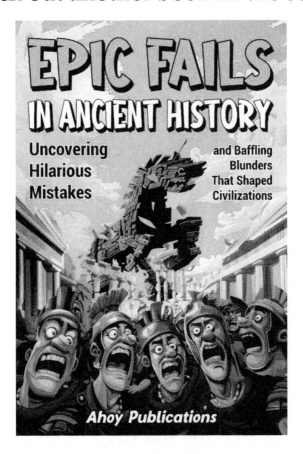

Welcome Aboard, Check Out This Limited-Time Free Bonus!

Ahoy, reader! Welcome to the Ahoy Publications family, and thanks for snagging a copy of this book! Since you've chosen to join us on this journey, we'd like to offer you something special.

Check out the link below for a FREE e-book filled with delightful facts about American History.

But that's not all - you'll also have access to our exclusive email list with even more free e-books and insider knowledge. Well, what are ye waiting for? Click the link below to join and set sail toward exciting adventures in American History.

Access your bonus here

https://ahoypublications.com/

Or, Scan the QR code!

References

3 Horrifying Facts of Renaissance Life. (2015, April 29). Inland 360. https://www.inland360.com/lewiston-moscow/3-horrifying-facts-of-renaissance-life/Content?oid=11374054

A Short History of the Web. (n.d.). CERN. https://home.cern/science/computing/birth-web/short-history-web

Abeza, D. (2022, January 30). 21 Interesting Michelangelo Facts That You Might Not Know. ATX Fine Arts. https://www.atxfinearts.com/blogs/news/michelangelo-facts

Adair, M. (2020, June 19). Bones in Churches, What's That About? Michael the Canadian. https://www.michaelthecanadian.com/blog/bones-in-churches-whats-that-about

Africa, H. (2019, May 31). The Ancient Egyptian Myth Where the God Atum Created the Universe by Masturbating to Ejaculation. Hadithi Africa | A Platform for the African Narrative; Hadithi Africa. https://hadithi.africa/the-ancient-egyptian-myth-where-the-god-atum-created-the-universe-by-masturbating-to-ejaculation/

Akhenaten, Nefertiti & Aten: From Many Gods to One. (2019, February 9). ARCE. https://arce.org/resource/akhenaten-nefertiti-aten-many-gods-one/

Altmeyer, S. (n.d.). Scientific Revolution. Colby.Edu. https://web.colby.edu/st112a-fall18/2018/09/21/3761/#more-3761

Andrews, E. (2014, March 4). 10 Things You May Not Know about Roman Gladiators. HISTORY. https://www.history.com/news/10-things-you-may-not-know-about-roman-gladiators

Andrews, E. (2015, March 6). 9 Things You May Not Know about Michelangelo. HISTORY. https://www.history.com/news/9-things-you-may-not-know-about-michelangelo

Arani, M. G., Fakharian, E., & Sarbandi, F. (2011). Ancient Legacy of Cranial Surgery. Archives of Trauma Research, 1(2), 72-74. https://doi.org/10.5812/atr.6556

Arts, G. (n.d.). 5 Surprising Facts about Leonardo Da Vinci. Google Arts & Culture. https://artsandculture.google.com/story/5-surprising-facts-about-leonardo-da-vinci/WwUB-Ph6UEWmuA?hl=en

Automata Through The Renaissance - the Mechanical Art & Design Museum. (2016, June 30). The Mechanical Art & Design Museum. https://themadmuseum.co.uk/history-of-automata/automata-through-the-renaissance/

Bahudodda, S. (n.d.). The Not-So-Scientific Revolution. Colby.Edu. https://web.colby.edu/st112a-fall18/2018/09/19/scientific-revolution-3/#more-3742

BBC News. (2014, February 14). 10 Bizarre Victorian Love Stories. BBC. https://www.bbc.com/news/magazine-26136764

Bio, M. (n.d.). Hieronymus Bosch. Thehistoryofart.org. https://www.thehistoryofart.org/hieronymus-bosch/

Bosch Paintings, Bio, Ideas. (n.d.). The Art Story. https://www.theartstory.org/artist/bosch-hieronymus/

Braun, A. (n.d.). Her Majesty's Rat-Catcher. Lapham's Quarterly. https://www.laphamsquarterly.org/roundtable/her-majestys-rat-catcher

Brigden, J. (n.d.). The Great Stink: London's Unbearable Summer of 1858. Sky HISTORY TV Channel. https://www.history.co.uk/articles/the-great-stink-londons-unbearable-summer-of-1858

Burton, E. (2020, May 9). Akhenaten: The Forgotten Pioneer of Atenism and Monotheism. TheCollector. https://www.thecollector.com/akhenaten-monotheism/

Carlton, G. (2019, January 4). The Creepiest Myths and Legends from Ancient Egypt. Ranker. https://www.ranker.com/list/creepy-myths-of-ancient-egypt/genevieve-carlton

Chandler, G. (2022, April 15). 15 Victorian Facts for kids. National Geographic Kids. https://www.natgeokids.com/uk/discover/history/general-history/victorian-facts/

Chao-Fong, L. (n.d.). Leonardo da Vinci: 10 Facts You Might Not Know. History Hit. https://www.historyhit.com/facts-you-might-not-know-about-leonardo-da-vinci/

Chavers, A. (2017, June 21). 43 Interesting (and Some Downright Weird) Facts about the Roman Emperors. Medium. https://medium.com/@achavers23/43-interesting-and-some-downright-weird-facts-about-the-roman-emperors-654ce363fb7b

Chen, A. (2017, April 6). Bison or Brian? From a Calorie Perspective, Cannibalism Didn't Pay for Paleo Humans. NPR. https://www.npr.org/sections/thesalt/2017/04/06/522880018/what-s-the-dietary-value-of-a-human

Daley, J. (2017, April 11). 13,000-Year-Old Fillings Were "Drilled" with Stone and Packed with Tar. Smithsonian Magazine. https://www.smithsonianmag.com/smart-news/researchers-find-filling-made-stone-age-dentist-180962845/

Devdiscourse News Desk. (2023, February 1). The Rise of Artificial Intelligence: Navigating the Future with AI. Devdiscourse.

https://www.devdiscourse.com/article/technology/2338982-the-rise-of-artificial-intelligence-navigating-the-future-with-ai

Did Nero Really Fiddle while Rome Burned? (2012, November 20). HISTORY. https://www.history.com/news/did-nero-really-fiddle-while-rome-burned

Dow, K. (2019). Looking into the Test Tube: The Birth of IVF on British Television. Medical History, 63(2), 189–208. https://doi.org/10.1017/mdh.2019.6

Duffy, C. (2023, April 27). How Elon Musk Upended Twitter and His Own Reputation in 6 Months as CEO. CNN. https://www.cnn.com/2023/04/27/tech/elon-musk-twitter-six-months/index.html

Frater, J. (2016, June 21). 10 Fascinating Facts about Rome's Vestal Virgins. Listverse. https://listverse.com/2016/06/21/10-fascinating-facts-about-romes-vestal-virgins/

Fun Facts about Michelangelo. (2023, February 15). The Art Post Blog | Art and Artists Italian Blog. https://www.theartpostblog.com/en/fun-facts-about-michelangelo/

George IV. (2018, October 18). Historic UK. https://www.historic-uk.com/HistoryUK/HistoryofBritain/George-IV/

Goodman, L. M. (n.d.). Who Is the Mysterious Bitcoin Creator Satoshi Nakamoto? Cointelegraph. https://cointelegraph.com/learn/who-is-satoshi-nakamoto-the-creator-of-bitcoin

Gualano, M. R., Bert, F., Gili, R., Andriolo, V., Scaioli, G., & Siliquini, R. (2015). The "Ice Bucket Challenge": Wondering about the Impact of Social Networks to Promote Public Health Interventions. Igiene e Sanita Pubblica, 71(4). https://pubmed.ncbi.nlm.nih.gov/26519744/

Hamilton, J. (2021, October 20). The Eye of Ra: The Meaning and Symbolism of this Ancient Egyptian Icon. MythBank. https://mythbank.com/eye-of-ra/

Handwerk, B. (2020, April 2). In Groundbreaking Find, Three Kinds of Early Humans Unearthed Living Together in South Africa. Smithsonian Magazine. https://www.smithsonianmag.com/science-nature/homo-erectus-australopithecus-saranthropus-south-africa-180974571/

Hapsara, I. V. W. (1596197154000). Viral Contents, Cyberbullying, and the Crowds Phenomenon. Linkedin.com. https://www.linkedin.com/pulse/viral-contents-cyberbullying-crowds-phenomenon-ignatius-vito

Harmes, M. (2022, June 7). Why Did People Start Eating Egyptian Mummies? The Weird and Wild Ways Mummy Fever Swept through Europe. The Conversation. http://theconversation.com/why-did-people-start-eating-egyptian-mummies-the-weird-and-wild-ways-mummy-fever-swept-through-europe-177551

He, A. (2022, July 27). Polarizing Remedies, Attractive Cures: Animal Magnetism, Mesmerism, and Mind-Over-Matter Treatments. Becker Medical Library. https://becker.wustl.edu/news/polarizing-remedies-attractive-cures-animal-magnetism-mesmerism-and-mind-over-matter-treatments/

Heritage History. (n.d.). Heritage-history.com. https://www.heritage-history.com/index.php?c=read&author=macgregor&book=rome&story=geese

History of the Web - World Wide Web Foundation. (2009, October 18). World Wide Web Foundation - Founded by Tim Berners-Lee, Inventor of the Web, the World Wide Web Foundation Empowers People to Bring about Positive Change; World Wide Web Foundation. https://webfoundation.org/about/vision/history-of-the-web/

Hoffenberg, R. (2001). Christiaan Barnard: His First Transplants and Their Impact on Concepts of Death. BMJ : British Medical Journal, 323(7327), 1478–1480. https://doi.org/10.1136/bmj.323.7327.1478

Hughes, D. (2018, June 25). The ALS Ice Bucket Challenge Phenomenon. Digital Marketing Institute. https://digitalmarketinginstitute.com/blog/viral-marketing-the-als-ice-bucket-challenge

In Vitro Fertilization (IVF). (2023, September 1). Mayoclinic.org. https://www.mayoclinic.org/tests-procedures/in-vitro-fertilization/about/pac-20384716

Johnson, S. (2017, July 19). King George IV and Mrs Fitzherbert. Downside Abbey. https://www.downsideabbey.co.uk/george-iv-mrs-fitzherbert/

Kashgar. (n.d.). The Bawdy Graffiti of Pompeii and Herculaneum. Kashgar. https://kashgar.com.au/blogs/history/the-bawdy-graffiti-of-pompeii-and-herculaneu

Katdevitt, P. by. (2020, August 31). Abode of Love: Home to a Wacky Victorian Sex Cult. Kat Devitt. https://katdevitt.com/2020/08/31/abode-of-love-home-to-a-wacky-victorian-sex-cult/

Kelly, D. B. (2017, September 14). Messed Up Things That Actually Happened in the Middle Ages. Grunge. https://www.grunge.com/86007/messed-things-actually-happened-middle-ages/

Kelly, D. B. (2018, August 10). Messed up Things That Actually Happened in the Victorian Era. Grunge. https://www.grunge.com/130940/victorian-era-messed-up-history/

Klein, C. (2022, August 12). 8 Fascinating Facts about Ancient Roman Medicine. HISTORY. https://www.history.com/news/ancient-roman-medicine-galen

LaFrance, A. (2016, March 29). The Graffiti at Pompeii. Atlantic Monthly (Boston, Mass.: 1993).

https://www.theatlantic.com/technology/archive/2016/03/adrienne-was-here/475719/

Leakey, L. (2018, January 12). Stone Age. HISTORY. https://www.history.com/topics/pre-history/stone-age

Leatherdale, D. (2019, February 9). Trial by Ordeal: When Fire and Water Determine Guilt. BBC. https://www.bbc.com/news/uk-45799443

Lesso, R. (2022, March 1). Why Did the Renaissance Start in Italy? TheCollector. https://www.thecollector.com/why-did-the-renaissance-start-in-italy/

Lillywhite, M. (2023, February 5). 5 Weird Things That Were Normal in Ancient Rome. Lessons from History. https://medium.com/lessons-from-history/5-weird-things-that-were-normal-in-ancient-rome-18267a70442f

Long, T. (2008, January 4). Jan. 4, 1903: Edison Fries an Elephant to Prove His Point. Wired. https://www.wired.com/2008/01/dayintech-0104/

Mann, E. (2016, April 4). Story of Cities #14: London's Great Stink Heralds a Wonder of the Industrial World. The Guardian. https://www.theguardian.com/cities/2016/apr/04/story-cities-14-london-great-stink-river-thames-joseph-bazalgette-sewage-system

Margaritoff, M. (2023, April 22). Queen Nefertiti Was a Powerful Ruler in Ancient Egypt — Until She Mysteriously Disappeared. All That's Interesting. https://allthatsinteresting.com/nefertiti

Mark, J. J. (2014). Nefertiti. World History Encyclopedia. https://www.worldhistory.org/Nefertiti/

Mark, J. J. (2018). Roman Empire. World History Encyclopedia. https://www.worldhistory.org/Roman_Empire/

Metta, S., Madhavan, N., & Krishnamoorthy Narayanan, K. (2022). Power of 280: Measuring the Impact of Elon Musk's Tweets on the Stock Market. Ushus Journal of Business Management, 21(1), 17–43. https://doi.org/10.12725/ujbm.58.2

Meyer, I. (2021, August 31). Michelangelo Facts - 12 Things to Know about Michelangelo. Artincontext.org; artincontext. https://artincontext.org/michelangelo-facts/

Mitchell, R. (2022, November 27). 10 Shocking Facts about the Ancient Romans. Ancient Origins. https://www.ancient-origins.net/history-ancient-traditions/shocking-roman-facts-0017584

Mitchell, R. (2022, September 13). Medieval Divorce by Combat: Guaranteeing 'til Death Do Us Part.' Ancient Origins Reconstructing the Story of Humanity's Past; Ancient Origins. https://www.ancient-origins.net/history-ancient-traditions/divorce-combat-0017263

Molecular Expressions: Science, Optics and You - Timeline - Zacharias Janssen. (n.d.). Fsu.Edu. https://micro.magnet.fsu.edu/optics/timeline/people/janssen.html

Mussio, G. (2015, July 8). 8 Interesting Facts about Michelangelo That Might Surprise You. Walksofitaly.com. https://www.walksofitaly.com/blog/art-culture/interesting-facts-about-michelangelo

Nix, E. (2016, June 21). Did Caligula Really Make His Horse a Consul? HISTORY. https://www.history.com/news/did-caligula-really-make-his-horse-a-consul

O'Carroll, S. (2013, February 16). The History of the Two-Headed Dog Experiment. The Journal.Ie. https://www.thejournal.ie/two-headed-dogs-794157-Feb2013/

Osiris. (n.d.). Cliffsnotes.com. https://www.cliffsnotes.com/literature/m/mythology/summary-and-analysis-egyptian-mythology/osiris

Parshina-Kottas, Y., Singhvi, A., Burch, A. D. S., Griggs, T., Gröndahl, M., Huang, L., Wallace, T., White, J., & Williams, J. (2021, May 24). What the 1921 Tulsa Race Massacre Destroyed. The New York Times. https://www.nytimes.com/interactive/2021/05/24/us/tulsa-race-massacre.html

Pepi II and the Dwarf. (2014, June 17). Discovering Ancient Egypt. https://discoveringegypt.com/ancient-egyptian-kings-queens/pepi-ii-and-the-dwarf/

Red Scare. (2010, June 1). HISTORY. https://www.history.com/topics/cold-war/red-scare

Reilly, L. (2019, January 13). When Queen Victoria Employed an Official Rat-Catcher. Mental Floss. https://www.mentalfloss.com/article/91629/queen-victoria-employed-official-rat-catcher

Romano, A. (2021, March 31). Satanic Panic's Long History — and Why It Never Really Ended — Explained. Vox. https://www.vox.com/culture/22358153/satanic-panic-ritual-abuse-history-conspiracy-theories-explained

Schiffer, Z., Newton, C., & Heath, A. (2023, January 17). Inside Elon Musk's "Extremely Hardcore" Twitter. The Verge. https://www.theverge.com/23551060/elon-musk-twitter-takeover-layoffs-workplace-salute-emoji

Scientific Breakthroughs of the Enlightenment that Changed our World. (n.d.). IMNOVATION. https://www.imnovation-hub.com/society/scientific-breakthroughs-enlightenment/

Serene Musings. (n.d.). Blogspot.com. http://serene-musings.blogspot.com/2010/10/boy-king-governor-and-dwarf.html

Simon, M. (2014, September 24). Fantastically Wrong: Europe's Insane History of Putting Animals on Trial and Executing Them. Wired. https://www.wired.com/2014/09/fantastically-wrong-europes-insane-history-putting-animals-trial-executing/

Sonia, P. (n.d.). 10 Crazy Things the Ancient Romans Actually Did. The Day Creek Howl. https://daycreekhowl.org/3765/arts-entertainment/10-crazy-things-the-ancient-romans-actually-did/

Stańska, Z. (2023a, April 15). 11 Things You Might Not Know about Leonardo da Vinci. DailyArt Magazine. https://www.dailyartmagazine.com/11-things-you-might-not-know-about-leonardo-da-vinci/

Stańska, Z. (2023b, August 13). 10 Facts You Didn't Know about Michelangelo. DailyArt Magazine. https://www.dailyartmagazine.com/facts-didnt-know-michelangelo/

Stewart, J. (2022, February 14). 14 Facts About Leonardo da Vinci's Incredible Life. My Modern Met. https://mymodernmet.com/leonardo-da-vinci-facts/

Stonewall Riots. (2017, May 31). HISTORY. https://www.history.com/topics/gay-rights/the-stonewall-riots

The Creation. (n.d.). Cliffsnotes.com. https://www.cliffsnotes.com/literature/m/mythology/summary-and-analysis-egyptian-mythology/the-creation

The Great Stink - A Victorian Solution to the Problem of London's Waste. (n.d.). Org.uk. https://historicengland.org.uk/images-books/archive/collections/photographs/the-great-stink/

The Life of Dolly. (n.d.). Ed.ac.uk.

The Life of Gladiators in Rome. (n.d.). Omnia Rome and Vatican Pass. https://romeandvaticanpass.com/en-us/blog/the-life-of-gladiators-in-rome

The Mystery of Unknown Man E - Archaeology Magazine Archive. (n.d.). Archaeology.org. https://archive.archaeology.org/0603/abstracts/mysteryman.html

The Rise of Beatlemania. (2022, November 19). Museum of Youth Culture. https://museumofyouthculture.com/beatlemania/

This Month in Archaeology: Three Different Early Humans Coexisted in South Africa ... Around 2 Million Years Ago. (n.d.). The Australian Museum. https://australian.museum/blog/amri-news/three-different-early-humans-coexisted-in-south-africa/

TIMESOFINDIA.COM. (2022, April 5). Five Times Elon Musk Changed the Rules with His Tweets. Times Of India. https://timesofindia.indiatimes.com/business/international-business/five-times-elon-musk-changed-the-rules-with-his-tweets/articleshow/90668461.cms

Top Unsolved Mysteries of Ancient Egypt. (2023, January 19). Egypt Tours Portal. https://www.egypttoursportal.com/blog/ancient-egyptian-civilization/top-unsolved-mysteries-of-ancient-egypt/

Turtle, M. (2017, May 15). Visiting the Sedlec Ossuary - Kutna Hora Bone Church! (2023). Time Travel Turtle. https://www.timetravelturtle.com/czech-republic/sedlec-ossuary-kutna-hora/

Vargas, C. (2018, January 4). 16 Fascinating Facts You Didn't Know about Queen Victoria. Town & Country. https://www.townandcountrymag.com/society/tradition/a14510744/queen-victoria-facts/

Vietnam War Protests. (2010, February 22). HISTORY. https://www.history.com/topics/vietnam-war/vietnam-war-protests

Waxman, O. B. (2019, January 4). Amelia Earhart Was Declared dead 80 years ago. Here's what to Know about What Actually Happened to Her. Time. https://time.com/5486999/amelia-earhart-disappearance-theories/

Weber, G. W., Lukeneder, A., Harzhauser, M., Mitteroecker, P., Wurm, L., Hollaus, L.-M., Kainz, S., Haack, F., Antl-Weiser, W., & Kern, A. (2022). The Microstructure and the Origin of the Venus from Willendorf. Scientific Reports, 12(1), 1–10. https://doi.org/10.1038/s41598-022-06799-z

White, F. (2019, September 23). 12 Bizarre Medieval Trends. Livescience.Com; Live Science. https://www.livescience.com/12-bizarre-medieval-trends.html

Why Thomas Edison and Nikola Tesla Clashed During the Battle of the Currents. (2021, May 13). Biography. https://www.biography.com/inventors/thomas-edison-nikola-tesla-feud

Wilford, J. N. (2009, June 24). Flutes Offer Clues to Stone-Age Music. The New York Times. https://www.nytimes.com/2009/06/25/science/25flute.html

Wong, H. (2019, September 20). The Secrets of the Victims of Mount Vesuvius. Pompeii Tours. https://www.pompeiitours.it/blog/the-secrets-of-the-victims-of-mount-vesuvius/

Young, L. J. (2018, February 6). The Real Scientific Revolution Behind "Frankenstein." Science Friday. https://www.sciencefriday.com/articles/real-scientific-revolution-behind-frankenstein/

Zarevich, E. (2022, December 13). Eleanor of Aquitaine's "Court of Love." JSTOR Daily. https://daily.jstor.org/eleanor-of-aquitaines-court-of-love/

Printed in Great Britain
by Amazon